Sound Before Symbol

A Lucky Duck Book

Sound Before Symbol

Developing Literacy through Music

Maria Kay

Los Angeles | London | New Delhi
Singapore | Washington DC

Los Angeles | London | New Delhi
Singapore | Washington DC

SAGE Publications Ltd
1 Oliver's Yard
55 City Road
London EC1Y 1SP

SAGE Publications Inc.
2455 Teller Road
Thousand Oaks, California 91320

SAGE Publications India Pvt Ltd
B 1/I 1 Mohan Cooperative Industrial Area
Mathura Road
New Delhi 110 044

SAGE Publications Asia-Pacific Pte Ltd
3 Church Street
#10-04 Samsung Hub
Singapore 049483

Editor: Miriam Davey
Production editor: Thea Watson
Proofreader: Jill Birch
Cover design: Wendy Scott
Typeset by: C&M Digitals (P) Ltd, Chennai, India
Printed in India at Replika Press Pvt Ltd

Library of Congress Control Number: 2012941635

British Library Cataloguing in Publication data

A catalogue record for this book is available from
the British Library

ISBN 978-1-4462-5246-8
ISBN 978-1-4462-5247-5 (pbk)

This book is dedicated to my mother, Marjorie Kay.
She has had unfaltering faith that I would complete it and
she has painstakingly read through the drafts countless times. It is without
doubt that her love of and interest in the English language and music
have been inspirational to my work in these mutually supportive areas.

Contents

Preface

The phrase 'sound before symbol' was coined by Carl Orff, a twentieth-century German composer and teacher, in order to illustrate that sound always precedes the introduction of its iconic representation. The ability to identify our profusion of sounds is vital to future literacy proficiency. Once the sounds of our language have been recognised by the brain, they can then be matched to their graphical equivalent – alphabetical characters.

There are many parallels that can be drawn between the skills promoted through music and those required for literacy development. It is possible to identify specific areas where parity may be observed in terms of the skills required in both fields.

I have set up and run many pre-school music groups and delivered workshops for parents and children to help children with literacy. I noticed over time, that the skills being developed through the musical activities were the same, in many cases, as those required for literacy and I undertook research into links between these two areas. This book is the result of my findings, observations and collation of research from other academic sources. The activities herein are mainly for early years children (aged 0–8 years as defined by the Children's Act 1989), but many may easily be adapted for use with older children.

The completion of my research resulted in the development of Sounds and Symbols, a unique literacy-through-music programme that presents musical activities from a literacy perspective with the purpose of eliciting literacy outcomes. It is specifically designed to equip pre-school children with the skills required for listening, speaking, reading and writing through a range of musical activities, thus securing a sound foundation for future literacy success. Many of the ideas used in the programme and others are detailed in this book.

The benefits of participating in musical activities are far-reaching, yet music is an area that is often sidelined. In 1998, I appeared on BBC local TV news advising on the importance of pre-school music to literacy development. Meredith (1998) reported that, 'there are fears that music is under threat, this evidence suggests that schools should be looking at ways to increase music rather than to cut back'. In 2012, the situation remained unchanged (Walters, 2012), with many councils in England and Scotland being under threat of cutbacks in their budgets for music services.

Fortunately there is much support from practitioners to oppose this retrograde step. For example, from Benedetti (Horne, 2011), Young Musician of the Year 2004, 'Councils don't realise that music lessons are not just an enjoyable extra. They're something that can do so much for morale, communication skills, learning, discipline and concentration and could actually save money for the future.' There is also mounting scientific evidence, for example that of Kraus and Chandrasekaran (2010), that the marginalisation of music training in schools should be reassessed. It should not be an optional extra. Music can provide an excellent vehicle for many aspects of child development. As propounded by Bolduc in his conclusion (2008), 'Music education offers a holistic type of education.'

Acknowledgements

My thanks are extended to my parents for their love and unconditional dedication to my happiness and wellbeing throughout my life, without which I would not have had the skills or motivation to complete this book.

I would like to express my gratitude also to my sons Jamie and Robbie Hickey and my partner Jaime Bryant, for their supply of patience, encouragement and support during the writing of the book. A special thank you, too, to Jaime for all of his technical help.

Many thanks are due to Lizzie Sharp, an extremely talented musician and teacher who has devoted many hours to the editing and correction of the music for this book, as well as for being a supportive friend. I have also much appreciated the help with the checking of the manuscript and support of my friend Jill Addison.

I am extremely grateful to Alicja Karp for providing the lovely graphics and Aleksandra Karp for kindly providing the artistic content.

Thanks also to the children who have learned with me and participated so readily in the songs, rhymes and games that I know today; most recently the children from the Jack and Jill Nursery in Elgin, Scotland, and those from Kestrel House, in Elgin, Scotland.

How to use this book

Each chapter is preceded by an outline of contents and is concluded by a short summary.

Suggestions for activities are given within each chapter in order to support their value to the various aspects of literacy and these are brought together in the final chapter to offer an examplar literacy-through-music programme.

At the end of each chapter are suggestions for 'Something to think about' and 'Something to read', along with details of websites of related interest.

A glossary is provided to clarify terminology; each item in the Glossary is high-lighted in the text when it is first mentioned.

Music is included in simple keys (C, D, G and F Major) in order to facilitate ease of playing.

For consistency, I have used the term 'teacher' throughout this book to refer to any leader of activities.

Activities

Figures and tables

Figures

Table

Key for icons

This chapter covers

Ideas

Activities

Summary

Something to think about

Something to read

Useful websites

About the author

 Maria Kay is the founder of Sounds and Symbols, a literacy-through-music pre-school activity programme. The programme is based on over thirty years' experience in education and was inspired by research undertaken whilst studying for a Masters in Education. This research was first reported on the BBC's regional TV news programme for the east of England 'Look East' in 1998. The Sounds and Symbols activity programme has since been delivered across the UK and abroad.

Maria has extensive experience in education. She has held various departmental head posts and several posts as an examiner and moderator. She has worked in many schools and colleges, most recently with pupils studying English as a second language and pupils with special educational needs.

Maria's teaching has included working with pre-school, primary school children and their parents to promote literacy through musical activities. She has devised and delivered family literacy programmes for Suffolk, Norfolk and Moray Councils.

Maria is an avid proponent of increasing musical provision throughout pre-school and primary curricula. She currently resides in Scotland, where she is promoting Sounds and Symbols worldwide.

If you would like to contact Maria or find out more about the Sounds and Symbols activity programme and training, please visit: http://soundsandsymbols.co.uk.

Introduction

Sound Before Symbol highlights the extensive world of early years musical activities and focusses in particular on the close relationship between music and literacy. By increasing awareness of the value of musical activities to literacy, I hope to encourage early years educators to make greater use of this substantial resource.

The National Literacy Trust (NLT), a UK charity, has found that one in six people in the UK struggle with literacy. The government is striving to improve the curriculum to create a fully literate nation. I believe that participation by early years children in musical activities can do much to contribute to the success of their future literacy ability.

Theorists agree that the early years (0–8 years of age) are the most formative on which the rest of life is constructed. This is the time when the brain is at its most **plastic** and much of what we learn in these years lays the foundation for who we are to become. It is important that we as parents and educators invest time and the right resources in order to maximise the potential of our children in their early years, to enable them to live full and productive lives.

According to Dryden and Vos (2005: 264), these eight years are 'the vital years' as, 'Up to 50 per cent of a person's ability to learn emerges by age four. Another 30 per cent may develop by the eighth birthday.'

Charles Darwin, the British scientist who laid the foundations for the theory of evolution, discovered that a challenging environment stimulates brain growth, so this is a time when we can greatly influence a child's development. Music provides a natural way to learn and to communicate. Children love songs, being sung to and singing themselves. Young children also revel in expending energy, not only in movement but in being creative and captivated by the exhilaration of learning. Playing instruments helps children to investigate how sounds are produced and how they can be made loud or quiet, long or short, high or low, fast or slow. Children may appreciate **timbre** by showing preference for one instrument over another as its sound may be warmer or stronger. Emotions may be investigated through music and children should be encouraged to describe how particular music makes them feel. Music clearly has a significant role to play in the development of young children.

Literacy development has always been foremost on the early years academic agenda. Without literacy, pathways for communication are reduced and future prospects impeded. Research by the NLT suggests that men and women with poor literacy skills are least likely to be in full-time employment at the age of thirty. This has serious implications for the productivity of the economy.

There are so many areas of overlap between the skills required for music and literacy, that it is almost indisputable – given the evidence herein – that participation in early musical activities enriches, complements and lays foundations for the development of literacy skills. Musical activities can be focussed in such a way as to elicit specifically the skills required for literacy. The literacy element does not need to be obvious but can be unobtrusively interwoven to render it almost subliminal. In this way the skills required for literacy can be established early and embedded for later use.

Chapter 1 considers the ways in which young children may experience music in their early years. It then examines the myriad of benefits that may be derived through this experience and demonstrates how music can support many areas of the early years curriculum.

Chapter 2 investigates how children may achieve competence in literacy and identifies the skills required in order to become literate. The methods employed to teach the skills of reading and writing both current and past are also discussed. The role of music in assisting the development of literacy skills is demonstrated through example activities.

Chapter 3 details some of the research that has been undertaken into the commonalities between music and literacy. It examines how these elements can be mutually supportive. There is evidence presented from musicians, psychologists, neurologists, scientists, educationalists and other researchers.

Chapter 4 examines how the brain develops and how it works to process music and literacy, drawing further parallels between the two areas. Music incites movement and this chapter also considers the role of movement in assisting brain function and how this may ultimately affect literacy.

Chapter 5 lists musical ideas for the attainment of the 'communication and language' and 'literacy' early learning goals of the National Curriculum. It also offers a culmination of many of the ideas that have been presented throughout the book as a suggested literacy-through-music programme for pre-school children. There are also additional ideas for older children.

This book is intended for anyone interested in early years education. It aims to encourage the inclusion of musical activities in educational settings and in the home. The activities presented are therefore easy to learn and deliver. Primarily, activities are provided for the non-musician but it is hoped too however that musicians may also find inspiration herein to use their talent to support the literacy development of young children.

One of the major obstacles to overcome with regard to using music in the literacy classroom in some cases, is the teachers' confidence in their own musical abilities. It is not necessary for a teacher to be a musician in order for children to benefit from the provision of musical activities. Music is fun, it is motivational and it brings people together as a cohesive group.

For anyone who feels that they may need extra encouragement to present musical activities, the following ideas are suggested:

- Enlist the help of someone else; working together can build confidence.

- Use pre-recorded music to sing along to; make sure that you are able to sing along to any music that you use beforehand. Practise at home.

- Use traditional tunes or those with which you are familiar.

- Learn the words.

- Practise any actions.

Woven through the book are details of over thirty musical activities that may be used to contribute to literacy skill development. I hope that you and the children you work with will enjoy them as much as I have.

The magic of music

This chapter covers

- What is music?

- Music before birth

- Music for babies

- The beneficial effects of music for young children

- The presentation of music to children in the early years

What is music?

It is important firstly to identify what is meant by music – almost any noise can be incorporated into musical composition, but sound alone cannot be defined as music.

Music has **structure**, pattern, sound, rhythm and variation in **pitch** – much the same as language. It can however be vocal or instrumental and there is a continuity of sound such that it becomes melodious and is generally pleasing to the ear.

Music can be made by using the body – humming, singing, whistling, stamping and clapping, or instruments which may be shaken, struck, blown, plucked, or bowed. Instruments may consist of conventional ones or unusual ones such as kitchen sinks or piping.

Young children may investigate music through:

Listening	Hearing and interpreting sounds
Composition	Exploration of sounds and putting these together in a sequence
Movement	Moving in response to sound
Performance	Making sounds
The printed score	To a limited extent. Although some children do learn to read musical notation at an early age, most do not. Through early music teaching children may be exposed to graphic notation.

Our first musical experience may well be from within the womb, listening to sounds from the outside world. These sounds may lay the foundation for our future development.

Music before birth

A consideration of musical activities for children raises the question, 'At what age can children begin to appreciate and benefit from music?' Are babies too young to learn through musical experiences?

Logan in the USA believes that babies begin to benefit from music from within the womb. Logan (in Logan et al., 1994) proposed that the first pattern that a child receives is that of the heartbeat. In his pursuit of enhancement of human performance, he proposed the concept of pre-natal stimulation. His Babyplus machine plays variations of a synthesised heartbeat to the foetus. On the Babyplus website it is proposed that, 'Babyplus babies are more relaxed and alert at birth, nurse better, are more self-soothing, reach their developmental milestones earlier and later in life are more school ready.'

At the same time in Moscow, Lazarev (in Logan et al., 1994) also developed a course of training for the unborn child. This was based on music rather than sounds and claimed to improve psychological development. Lazarev (2010) claimed that playing music to the unborn child helps to organise the developing foetal brain. He proposed that the naturally occurring death of the brain cells, prior to birth, (approximately half) is reduced by the playing of music to the foetus.

Hepper (in Logan et al., 1994) from Belfast was also studying the psychology of the foetus at this time. He believed that the foetus is capable of learning and proved this to be the case, by measuring response to stimuli after birth, which babies had also been exposed to whilst in the womb. The stimuli were tunes, which were played to babies before birth – their responses were measured by exposure to these after birth. Logan, Lazarev and Hepper each proposed that it is possible to influence a child's development before birth by stimulation of the brain using sound and/or music.

Babies in the womb can relax to external music and can become conditioned to respond similarly to the same music after birth. This is termed **'classical conditioning'**. Classical conditioning can occur from about five-and-a-half months after conception (Eliot, 2000).

Music for babies

A study in 2006 by Blumenfeld and Eisenfeld suggested that premature babies exposed to music – such as that of their mothers singing during feeding – have reduced symptoms of stress, faster weight gain and shorter stays in intensive care.

Kjaer (1993: 7) stated in her seminar paper that:

> If an educational programme based on music for the physical and mental development of children is already started when the children are under three years old, these children will be supported in their motor, sensory and linguistic functions, as well as in their social behaviour.

Kjaer supports the view that music can provide a valuable foundation for children and recognises its role in supporting linguistic skills as well as the importance of an early start. She also believes that a baby can recognise melodies played to the mother before birth, after it is born.

The way that a mother or indeed other adults or children speak to babies has been referred to as 'motherese'. It is usually higher in pitch than normal language, and is slower and more deliberate in its delivery and may contain shortened or simplified words. Although some people may think that this 'baby language' is childish and has little purpose, it does in fact help babies to assimilate language in an easier way than more adult speech. The research of Shore (1997) and others confirms this.

The rhythmic rocking, an almost subconscious activity when we hold a baby, is also beneficial to a child's development. Rocking is a soothing activity; it is natural, normal and necessary to our wellbeing. The rhythm in sound was studied by Schreckenberg and Bird in 1987 and they found that mice exposed to **arhythmic** beats, such as those in rock music, left the mice confused and incapacitated as the arhythmic beats disrupted the natural rhythmic patterns of the brain.

A study by Winkler et al. (2009) in Hungary showed that newborn babies develop expectation for the onset of rhythmic cycles (the downbeat). This supports the view that the perception of beat is inborn and not learned such that the capability of detecting beat is already functional at birth.

Goddard (2002: 108) describes music as a 'primary teacher' and says that, 'Before birth, the foetus reacts to music with changes in motor activity.' She believes that babies can imitate rhythms. She identifies melody recognition, language comprehension, picture recognition, spatial orientation and rhythm as skills that children need when starting to learn to read. She points out that music can be used to develop these skills in preparation for literacy.

There is much scientific evidence to demonstrate that music is beneficial to babies; it provides sound, rhythms and vibrations that can aid relaxation, this in turn enhances the ability to learn. Mothers have always used lullabies as a way to induce sleep for their babies. Music also provides stimulation to fire neural connections and can hone mental acuity.

So far it is possible to conclude that music for babies can be used to:

- aid relaxation

- promote alertness

- promote overall development

- stimulate the brain

- reduce stress

- support motor, linguistic, emotional functions and social behaviour

- help to emphasise the rhythm in language

- help the development of language and other literacy skills.

The beneficial effects of music for young children

A major effect of music is that it almost always elicits some form of response. Some of the beneficial effects that music is known to have on young children are as follows:

Relaxation

Relaxing music is often played when a calming effect is desired and it can help to promote thought and reflection. During relaxation the brain cells are able to work with greatest efficiency. When we are over-stressed, cortisol is produced. Cortisol is a hormone that causes the death of brain cells when we are over-stressed and we are unable to think clearly.

Stimulation

Music can be used to stimulate as well as relax. Loud and lively music can help us to let off steam. The Sufi music of the Whirling Dervishes assists the dervishes to go into a trance! Music can also be uplifting and motivational and can make us feel good. Music can cause mood change and has been reported to increase productivity at work. When the brain is stimulated, neurotransmitters fire causing connections to be made. Oldham et al. (1995) issued office workers with headphones through which they could listen to music. The researchers recorded a substantial increase in productivity of the workers who listened to music. This may well have a similar effect on children in the classroom.

Some people report that listening to music while they work is both enjoyable and helpful, whilst others, myself included, seem to block it out. Storr (1992: 111) suggests that, 'A perpetual background of good music to which little serious attention is paid diminishes both the music and the listener.' He adds that some intellectuals claim that their capacity for study is enhanced by background music but that there is also evidence that music interferes with intense concentration. It has also been suggested that maybe musical people 'tune in' more when listening to music than their non-musical counterparts. The music therefore becomes distracting instead of supportive. This is maybe due to the listener analysing the music rather than simply enjoying it.

 Idea

Play some background music of your choice and monitor the effect it has on the children you are working with. Ask the children how they feel about background music.

Imagination

Music can conjure up a world of imagination. Consider the backing music to films: without the music, would we be frightened in a horror movie or would we cry at an emotional scene? Music that we know and remember can stir up memories or music can lead us down new paths in our imagination, promoting inspiration and innovation.

Entertainment

Entertainment is possibly the greatest use of music. Music can be with us everywhere, at work, school, home, shops or as we travel; delivered through a wide range of electronic devices. 'Children are more likely to own a mobile phone than a book,' was a quotation in *The Telegraph* (Paton, 2010). It would seem that some children may listen to music, converse or read from a phone, rather than read a book. Lyrics as well as melodies can be inspirational or emotive. We can use music to support our mood or turn off from the rigours of a day.

Movement

Music can be **motoric**, it may incite us to move – it may make us want to dance or sing or merely tap along. Much folk music evokes a desire to move, as of course does popular disco music. If we dance without music, we are almost compelled to hum or at least **subvocalise** a tune. Listening and moving to music is also associated with healing, improved intellect, alteration of brain states and **entrancement**.

Programmes which have been developed to encourage learning through music and movement include Braindance and Braingym. Where physical exercise is combined with enriched experience, a larger impact is made on the developing brain, especially while there is still **plasticity** in childhood. Exercise provides cognitive as well as physical benefits and enhances the rate of learning. Another programme, Write Dance uses music and movement to help children to develop handwriting skills.

 Idea

When selecting music for children, incorporate action songs and those with a strong rhythm that is easy to follow. This helps children to appreciate the rhythm in language.

Participation

Whether as an observer or an active participator, children love to be involved in musical activities. Music can encourage participation and can help to develop social skills.

Language and communication

Music can be used to provide a means of language and communication for children. It is often used in music therapy for communication with children who have no speech. Before children learn to speak, music can help to train their listening skills. Through listening, children are able to then imitate the sounds that they hear in order to produce language of their own. Children may sing before they can speak, this will certainly help to develop their vocalisation skills. Music can help to encourage sound making, both with the voice and with instruments.

Music is a form of expression that can be accessed by all. The system Soundbeam is one specially designed to enable children with profound and complex needs to create a wealth of musical sound without requiring fine motor or vocal skills. Any movement that is made can be transformed into sound by the 'sound beams'. Sound is always activated by movement and an area that links well with the science curriculum. Music is often used with children with learning difficulties where it can help pupils to communicate and express themselves. The Nordoff Robbins charity is one of many that use music therapy to transform the lives of children and adults. There was a report (Smith, 2012) in a national newspaper, of a non-verbal, autistic man who recorded an album after having music therapy. After a lifetime of silence he is now able to express himself through music.

Considering that many foreign children are often excellent at learning to speak English, I have often wondered why this is so. I believe that one reason for this accomplishment is the fact that many foreign children listen to English music. Hence, the sound patterns and vocabulary of the English language are established early on. The ability of the developing brain to make connections diminishes in some areas with time and cannot be recovered, one such area being language. There is a critical period for the ability to discriminate foreign speech sounds that lasts only for about the first six months of life. It therefore seems very likely that listening to music in foreign tongues, while very young, may help to facilitate later foreign language acquisition.

Activities 1.1, 1.2 and 1.3 make use of a traditional song that is easy and fun to perform. The lyrics can be found online in many languages. It is given here in English and Spanish with directions for signing. Look at how the note values reflect the **syllables** differently in English and Spanish. If children clap along to the rhythm, they will be able to physically sound out the syllables. This in turn will help them to **internalise** the breaking down of words and to develop **phonological awareness**. Ultimately this will help children with both reading and writing.

Activity 1.1   My Hat It Has Three Corners (song)

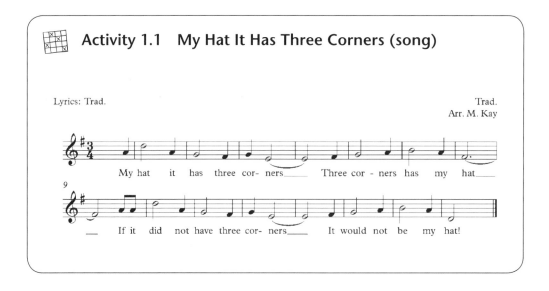

Activity 1.2   Mi Gorro Tiene Tres Picos (song)

Lyrics: Trad.

Trad.
Arr. M. Kay

Mi gor-ro ti - en - e tres pi- cos___ Tres pi-cos ti - en - e mi gor-ro

ro, Si no tu-vi - e - ra tres pi- cos___ Ya no se - rí - a mi gor-ro.

Activity 1.3   My Hat It Has Three Corners
(using hand signs)

Perform the song using hand signs as follows:

My – point to your own chest with one finger

Hat – raise a flat hand up and down above your head

Three – show three fingers

Corners – bend one hand in towards your chest and move elbow up and down

Did not/would not – with one hand push away to the side and shake your head

Performing these actions without actually singing aloud usually results in the performer 'singing' the words inside their head – 'internalising'.

Whilst listening to music in foreign tongues may help to familiarise us with other languages, listening to music in our own language will clearly assist the development of our native language, too. It can help to improve vocabulary, enunciation, comprehension and an appreciation of language structure.

Learning with music and Mozart

In 1993, Shaw and Rauscher of the University of California, Irvine (in Shaw, 1999), researched the effect of listening to Mozart. They found that listening to the music of Mozart caused a short-term improvement in spatial-temporal reasoning (the ability to visualise something over time, like the unfolding of a piece of paper). They termed this The Mozart Effect. This is now well documented.

Savan (1999), a science teacher, studied the effects of background music on learning. She played Mozart orchestral music in the classroom to a group of boys aged

12+ with behavioural and emotional problems and discovered that it improved coordination and behaviour. Babies in Scotland were able to sample the 'Mozart Effect' through free music CDs, from October 2012–2013, with funds from Creative Scotland, with the aim of enhancing early learning (Simpson, 2012).

Memory

It is possible that music can enhance memory retention. Webb and Webb (1990: 308) describe music as 'the interstate highway to the memory system'. Music can certainly help to evoke memories and facilitate recall. Often, if we hear a piece of music, it reminds us of where we were when we first or last heard it. We can 'hear' music that is not even present. This can be referred to as '**inner hearing**', hearing music in the head. It is the same to hearing as visualising is to seeing. I have previously referred to this process as 'internalising'. Gordon (1979), a music education researcher, coined the term '**audiation**' as a more extensive term to include 'thinking and comprehending' the music in addition to 'hearing'. The facility to imagine music in this way is important as it helps us to learn and remember how a song or piece of music should sound. This in turn helps us to reproduce the sound either vocally or instrumentally.

A traditional song for children that may be used to help the development of inner hearing and also introduces children to alphabetic letter names is shown in Activity 1.4.

 Activity 1.4   Bingo (song)

There was a farmer had a dog and Bingo was his name 'O'

B-I-N-G-O, B-I-N-G-O, B-I-N-G-O and Bingo was his name 'O'.

The same verse is sung six times. For the first verse, instead of singing the letter name, 'B' the letter is silent, children can clap instead of singing the letter. The second time 'B' and 'I' are silent, the third time 'B', 'I' and 'N' and so on. When all the letters have been silent, the final verse can be sung with all of the letters enunciated. The music for this song can be downloaded from http://www.soundsandsymbols.co.uk. Performing this song also helps concentration as the performers need to remember how many letters were omitted in the previous verse.

Singing in **rounds** helps children to focus and to hold the melody and lyrics in their heads. In a round, two or more groups sing the same words and the same song but start at differing times. Well-known songs that can be sung in this way are, London's Burning, Row, Row, Row Your Boat, I Hear Thunder and Frère Jacques.

Behaviour

Roskam (1993), a music therapist and teacher, discusses the influence of music on behaviour in her book *Feeling the Sound*. She discusses the impact of the power of music on the individual and groups and its positive and negative effects.

All the above responses to music can be utilised to motivate children in many different areas of learning, encouraging them to think, move, laugh, sing, sleep and be creative.

In conclusion, music for young children can be used to:

- promote relaxation/stimulation

- reduce stress

- fire the imagination

- provide entertainment

- induce movement

- encourage participation

- promote language and communication skills

- help foreign-language acquisition

- assist learning

- teach syllabification

- enhance memory

- influence behaviour.

The presentation of music to children in the early years

A child's first initiation into the 'language' of music may be prior to birth, hearing sounds that the mother is listening to or making; after birth the child may hear a variety of music that the mother also listens to, or music that the mother plays for the child, such as recorded nursery rhymes or her own singing. Many adults instinctively sing to babies, making soft, soothing sounds or rhymes to elicit response.

Private provision

Pre-school music groups

There are many pre-school music groups that are privately run. Participation in the musical activities of a group enables young children to learn by observation and by trial, experimenting with sound. If children attend pre-school music groups then they will be exposed to a variety of musical sounds and the concepts of **duration**, **dynamics**, **tempo**, **texture**, timbre, pitch and structure. They will learn to keep time by maintaining a beat or rhythm as well as by singing, performing action rhymes and moving to music. They may also learn some musical notation. They will usually also be introduced to instruments, which generally take the form of percussion instruments (homemade or bought), these being easy to 'play'. By using untuned instruments there is no fear of striking a wrong note as there can be no discordant sound.

Using a simple song such as that in Activity 1.5 assists in the development of rhythm, rhyme, syllabification, dynamics, tempo and memory retention. Lyrics may be varied for specific purposes, to accompany a theme or to practise rhyming skills. Playing along to the rhythm and taking turns with instruments help the development of language and social skills, too.

 Activity 1.5   I Hear Thunder (song)

Use the traditional tune to Frère Jacques

I hear thunder, I hear thunder (use drums and play loudly)

Hark don't you? Hark don't you?

Pitter, patter raindrops, pitter, patter raindrops (use rain sticks and sing and play quietly)

I'm wet through, you are too.

Clouds are floating, clouds are floating (sing and play all instruments slowly)

Through the sky, through the sky

Look! Here comes the sunshine. Look! Here comes the sunshine (sing and play all instruments quickly)

Please don't cry, we'll soon dry.

 Idea

My advice when buying instruments for pre-school children is to ensure that they are safe. They need to be strong and solid. Some beaters, for example those provided with metal triangles, may be unsuitable for children under three years of age. Do not buy cheap, insubstantial 'toy' instruments as these may fall apart and small pieces may present a choking hazard. When making instruments such as shakers, ensure that lids to containers are securely fixed so as not to release any contents. Percussion instruments in wood are usually ideal as they tend to have rounded edges. Plastic beaters may be sharp and easily broken.

In a pre-school music group, social skills are developed by children being with their peers and working alongside adults. Children learn to share and to appreciate the actions and desires of others as well as their own. They can learn how to express their emotions and to recognise those of others. They can investigate their feelings and experience and respond in a safe and caring environment.

Being encouraged and praised when participating, engenders a feeling of worth and acceptance. Being listened to and listening to others is an important part of music making. Children learn that they have a voice and that it is worthy of attention, also that they should listen to others, too. A feeling of belonging and of being included is important and of being part of a group. Each member has a role to play. During music group activities, children are encouraged to interact and to practise their communication skills.

Idea

Attend a pre-school music session and ask the leader if they could share ideas with you. This is how I was first inspired to start a music group and I am much indebted to that individual music teacher. Select activities that you are comfortable with. Do not be over-ambitious at the start.

 Idea

Take along props such as a puppet to 'speak' to the children. Children may respond more readily to a puppet than to an adult. Children may also be encouraged to speak through a puppet. Use dowels to make claves for tapping rhythms. Use ribbons or scarves for writing in the air or making patterns to music. Use props to support a selection of songs on a theme, for example use small hoops as steering wheels for transport songs or finger mice for mice rhymes.

Pre-school music groups provide activities that support the development of many skills for early years children. Music is a lovely medium through which to present a wide range of learning opportunities. For example, Activity 1.6 helps children to learn the days of the week and helps to introduce the concept of structure.

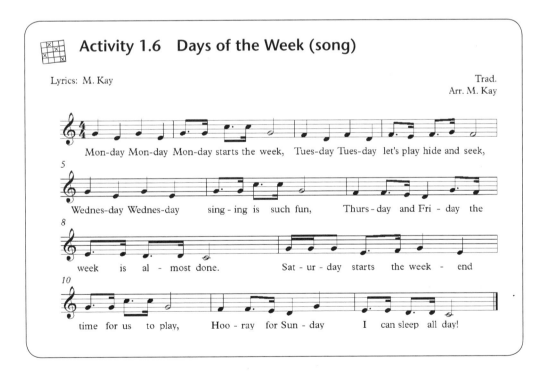

Activity 1.6   Days of the Week (song)

The structure of a music session itself is important. Activities should be varied but include the same songs to indicate the introduction or closing of activities each time. This helps children to learn to anticipate what is going to happen next. 'Hello' and 'goodbye' songs can be used to signal the beginning and ending of sessions. Also, songs specific to particular activities can be used to indicate what will happen next. For an example, see the song in Activity 1.7.

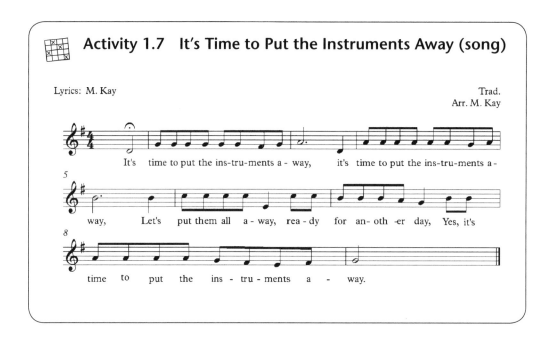

Popular methodologies

Another way in which children may access music and music tuition is by attendance at private provision that may subscribe to the philosophies and methods of well-known musicians and educators such as those of Kodály, Suzuki, Orff and Dalcroze.

Some children learn to play instruments from a very young age. Violins, for example, may be played by small children as they are available in many sizes. Children can often play a tune on a piano or keyboard once they have been shown the order of the notes, although caution should be exercised with regard to the physical toll on developing bones before young children spend excessive amounts of time playing an instrument.

Guiding

Music is also part of other extracurricular activities for young children such as Guiding. Rainbows, Brownies, Beavers and Cubs traditionally sing 'campfire' songs. You can find songs such as Quartermaster's Store, On Top of Spaghetti, Three Little Angels and We are the Redmen on the Guiding website.

Youth Music

The government-funded Youth Music Initiative has run several programmes to support early years staff and parents since the First Steps programme in 2000. The Music Start programme ran from 2007 to 2008 to encourage families with children aged 2–5 years of age to make music at home.

Music in the National Curriculum (NC): pre-school

The Pre-school Learning Alliance (PLA) has long advocated the incorporation of musical sessions in playgroups. Mother and toddler groups, playgroups and nurseries usually include musical activities in their sessions.

In government-run nurseries and in schools, the National Curriculum (NC) is delivered throughout the UK. Each country within the UK adapts the curriculum to its own requirements. The curriculum for pre-school (0–5 years) is thus prescribed by the country's respective educational body. In 2012, these were the bodies responsible for each country in the UK:

- England: Department for Education (DFE), the government department responsible for education from 2010 (replaced the Department for Children, Schools and Families (DCSF))

- Scotland: Learning and Teaching Scotland (part of 'Education Scotland')

- Wales: Department for Education and Skills

- Northern Ireland: Department of Education

In England, the Early Years Foundation Stage (EYFS), a legal requirement under the auspices of the Childcare Act 2006 is a comprehensive framework that was published in 2007 by the Department for Children, Schools and Families (DCSF) that became statutory in September 2008. The Statutory Framework for EYFS set standards for the development, learning and care of children from birth to five years and applies to all formal childcare settings. The 2008 EYFS had six equally important areas. In September 2012, these were replaced by a new Statutory Framework for the EYFS (DFE, 2012a). The changes were implemented as a result of the recommendations from the review by Dame Clare Tickell in 2011. She recommended a simplification of the learning and development requirements by reducing the number of early learning goals from 69 to 17. Of the seven identified areas of learning and development, greater weight was placed upon the 'prime areas' than the 'specific areas'.

The essence of the overarching principles remains unchanged from the 2008 guidelines but a summary of the rewording in the 2012 framework is 'every child is unique, children learn to be strong through positive relationships, children learn and develop well in enabling environments and children develop and learn in different ways and at different rates' (DFE, 2012a: 3).

In the 2012 EYFS framework (DFE, 2012a), 'literacy' became a separate area, making *seven areas of learning and development*, which were identified as '*prime*' or '*specific*' areas.

The *prime* areas are:

- communication and language

- physical development and

- personal, social and emotional development.

The *specific* areas are:

- literacy

- mathematics

- understanding the world and

- expressive arts and design.

Each of the seven areas of learning can be addressed through musical activities.

Communication and language

This area of learning and development is further divided into 'listening and attention', 'understanding' and 'speaking'. The guidance material *Development Matters in the Early Years Foundation Stage* (Early Education, 2012), illustrates what may be observed from children at various ages and suggests how adults can support this development by the activities and environments that they provide. Reference is made to the use of rhymes, stories, songs and pictures. The use of variety of tone and intonation in the voice is advised and the use of sounds from other cultures. Children need to hear and enjoy rhythmic patterns in rhymes, stories and songs.

Music is a form of expression and can be used to encourage communication. The activity programme for babies Sing and Sign provides one example of how music can help to support the learning of a communication system. Songs can convey emotion and can tell elaborate stories that are often easily recalled once the tune is called to mind.

Communication skills are encouraged through musical activities via imitation, singing, listening and making sounds. Children learn appropriate intonation, dynamics and vocabulary by listening to, copying and responding to the sounds that they hear. Encouraging children to echo melodies using lots of repetition helps children to embed sounds for later recall.

Physical development

Music helps to induce movement and children can develop fine and gross motor skills through musical activities.

A rhyme to practise a variety of movements to is Can You Tiptoe? (Activity 1.8). Recite the rhyme and move along according to the lyrics. Also, speak quietly when tiptoeing and lengthen the word 'fly' when being a bat; accentuate the marching rhythm for the soldier and use a fast, squeaky voice for the scampering rat.

 Activity 1.8   Can You Tiptoe? (rhyme)

Can you tiptoe like a cat?

Can you fly like a bat?

Can you march like a soldier?

Can you scamper like a rat?

Lyrics: M. Kay

Personal, social and emotional development (PSED)

Covered in this area is participation in groups, learning how to relate to peers and how to communicate and cooperate within a group. Music group activities help to foster the development of all three aspects of personal, social and emotional development (PSED) – building relationships, increasing self-confidence and self-awareness and managing feelings and behaviour. Musical stories and symbolic play can help to support this area of the curriculum.

Included in this area is '**emotional literacy**', the ability to recognise, understand and appropriately express our emotions. Emotions may be investigated through music; we are able to tell whether a piece of music is happy or sad. Listening to music may cause our emotional state to alter. Musical activities offer a wonderful opportunity for socialising and can provide a vehicle for self-expression.

Using the melody for the song It's Time to Put the Instruments Away (Activity 1.7), sing the lyrics in Actvity 1.9 and perform appropriate actions.

 Activity 1.9   If You're Pleased and You Know It (song)

Verse 1: If you're pleased and you know it, do thumbs up! (x 2)

If you're pleased and you know it and you really want to show it!

If you're pleased and you know it, do thumbs up!

Verse 2: If you're sad and you know it, do thumbs down!

Verse 3: If you're brave and you know it, stand up tall!

Verse 4: If you're scared and you know it, run away!

Verse 5: If you're great and you know it, shout 'I'm amazing!'

Substitute the lyrics appropriately for each verse.

Literacy

In this area children are required to use phonic knowledge to decode regular words. Music can help in the development of phonological awareness – the sound structure of words. Helping children to recognise rhymes, syllables and letter sounds within words is a first step in nurturing the skills that will eventually enable them to decode words. An awareness of variations in sound is imperative to the successful development of literacy skills.

Mathematics

Children are able to meet numerical concepts through music, to investigate how problems may be solved and to investigate cause and effect.

There are lots of counting songs, the lyrics and tunes for which are readily available on the Internet, such as: Five Currant Buns in a Baker's Shop, Ten Fat Sausages Sizzling in a Pan, Five Little Men in a Flying Saucer and Five Little Monkeys Jumping on the Bed. Use these to help children to appreciate the sequence of numbers and to learn '**The oneness of one**'.

Understanding the world

Songs can be informative and can be used to help children to understand and remember difficult concepts and the sequence of events.

The song Creepy Crawly Caterpillar (Activity 1.10) helps children to understand the process of metamorphosis. The use of a suitable prop such as a reversible puppet (caterpillar to butterfly) or pictures, helps to further embed the memory of the life-cycle process.

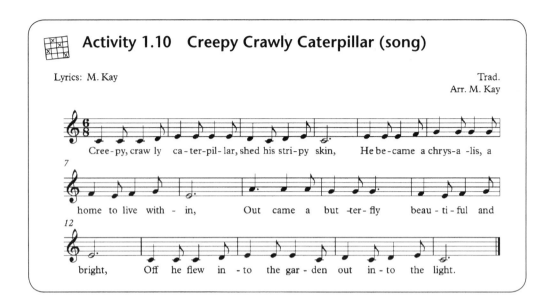

Activity 1.10   Creepy Crawly Caterpillar (song)

Lyrics: M. Kay

Trad.
Arr. M. Kay

Cree-py, craw ly ca-ter-pil-lar, shed his stri-py skin, He be-came a chrys-a -lis, a home to live with - in, Out came a but -ter- fly beau - ti - ful and bright, Off he flew in - to the gar - den out in - to the light.

Expressive arts and design

Music is expressly referred to in this area and the early learning goals are deter-mined as follows.

Exploring and using media and materials: children sing songs, make music and dance, and experiment with ways of changing them. They safely use and explore a vari-ety of materials, tools and techniques, experimenting with colour, design, texture, form and function (DFE, 2012a: 9).

Being imaginative: children use what they have learned about media and materials in original ways, thinking about uses and purposes. They represent their own ideas, thoughts and feelings through design and technology, art, music, dance, role-play and stories (DFE, 2012a: 9).

The other countries in the UK generally cover the same or very similar areas in their early years curricula.

Music can provide a medium through which children can:

- develop their physical and mental strength

- use musical activities to help provide a sense of belonging

- build confidence

- develop a sense of self and provide an arena where a child can be listened to and valued.

Music in the National Curriculum: primary school

As children enter school their music curriculum is under the directives of the gov-ernment Department for Education (DFE). There are stages through which children should progress, the first of these being Key Stage (KS) One (DFE, 2012b). This is covered in years 1 and 2, generally for children aged 5–7 years.

In Music at KS One of the NC (DFE, 2012b), children are expected to use their voices to make songs, chants and rhymes, play instruments and perform with others, and to create musical patterns, to listen to, internalise and recall sounds. Children learn about pitch, duration, dynamics, timbre, texture and silence and how sounds can be described using invented signs and symbols.

When children first begin to learn to read music they may be introduced to symbols to represent times when the instrument or sound should be played (this is termed 'graphic notation') . This could be a pictorial representation of their instrument or a teacher may use hand symbols. Concepts such as loud and quiet may be symbolised by a large picture for loud and a small one for quiet. An example is given in Figure 1.1.

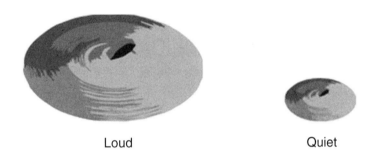

Loud   Quiet

Figure 1.1   Symbols to Represent 'Loud' and 'Quiet' Sounds

Using graphic notation children can also be encouraged to write their own music. It is something of an anomaly that whilst the term 'literacy' when applied to language refers to both reading and writing (plus listening and speaking), the term 'musical literacy' usually refers only to the ability to read music.

On paper, children can use symbols to illustrate the types of sounds that they wish to play. They may have several instruments and then pictures of each to represent the order in which the instruments are to be played. In addition to indicating loud and quiet, symbols may be elongated or truncated to represent long or short sounds, for example by a snake for a long sound and a mouse for a short one. An example is given in Figure 1.2.

Short   **Short**   **Long**

Figure 1.2   Symbols to Represent 'Short' and 'Long' Sounds

Activity 1.11   Graphic Notation

Using symbols as above, cards could be made up of various combinations. An example worksheet is provided below. In pairs, one child chooses and plays a rhythm from the list. The second child then guesses which rhythm has been played. The children then swap roles.

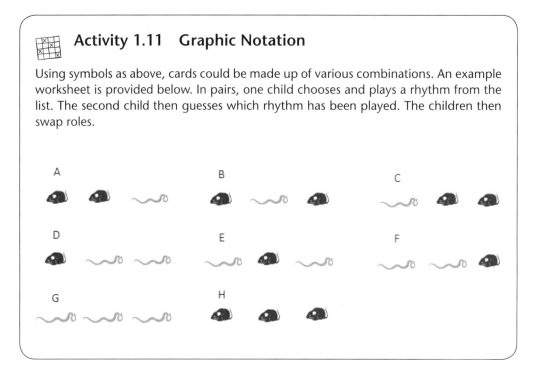

Reading and playing sounds helps children to develop **bibliographic knowledge**, an understanding that sound may be represented visually and that reading moves across the page from left to right and from top to bottom. This is not true for all languages. In Arabic, writing moves from right to left and Chinese traditionally was read in vertical columns from right to left and top to bottom.

Alternatively, compositions can be made using pictures to denote the instruments used and their frequency of play. For example, three shakes of a maraca would be represented pictorially by three maracas. Children can write their own music in this way.

Other symbols can be used such as rungs on ladders or sloping lines to indicate rise and fall in pitch.

As children progress, the mice and snakes can be replaced with conventional musical notation. Create different rhythms using crotchets, quavers and minims. Children could create and play their own rhythms. Rhythms could be performed with various body or percussion instruments.

Crotchet (1 beat)   Quavers (2 x half a beat)   Minim (2 beats)

Figure 1.3   Musical Note Names and Time Values

Idea

The teacher could ask the children how they might move to these rhythms. To further demonstrate these note values, each note could have an alliterative name, for example Katy Crotchet, Quickie Quaver and Moody Minim. The teacher could have puppets of the same name and each could be described. Katy Crotchet would walk at a walking (andante) pace. Quickie Quaver would move quickly (allegro) and Moody Minim would move with long, slow movements (lento). These musical terms are Italian, as is the word 'tempo' meaning 'time'. Many musical terms are Italian as most early composers in the Renaissance period were Italian. These terms were thereafter adopted internationally.

There are some very creative music reading ideas for children such as using animal pictures for each note, Noteimals by Glenna Cook, or using colour to code the notes. Colour-coding notes works well; I have used it with great success with children with learning difficulties. One system that uses colour and shape is Figurenotes, developed in Finland. It is used by Drake Music, Scotland, helping children and adults with disabilities to read, create and perform music.

As with pre-school music, primary school music can support many parts of the curriculum. Reference is made in KS One Music of the NC (DFE, 2012b) to links between music and English, Information Communications Technology (ICT), drama, physical education (PE) and science. For example, songs and rhymes can be sung in different languages; listening to and performing music helps children to learn to identify changes in sound such as those used in language. Movement to music would also be part of a drama curriculum, encouraging expression and communication. In PE, movement to music may help to develop body and spatial awareness. Music could help to embed other concepts such as those in science. Additionally, the making of instruments would cover art and creative development and rhymes, chants and songs can be used as reinforcement in maths, such as the chanting of multiplication tables.

External to the NC there are various initiatives available to support music making. One government-funded programme, Sing Up, invested £4 million over four years from 2007 in order to promote singing in primary schools in the UK and there are many Youth Music Projects supporting extracurricular music, too. The Sing Up website in 2012 had many examples of songs in English and foreign languages for use with primary school children.

Encouragingly, there is growing support for the implementation of increased music provision in the early years and primary school curricula. In addition to the support such as that from Benedetti (in Horne, 2011) and Kraus and Chandrasekaran (2010), referred to earlier in the Preface, there are many others championing the cause, including Henley and Norman, detailed below.

- Darren Henley's review on *Music Education in England* recommended that 'singing should be an important part of every child's school life from Early Years' (2011: 11). He also recommended that: 'A new minimum number of hours of Initial Teacher Training for primary music teachers be spent on the delivery of music education and that all primary schools should have access to a specialist music teacher' (ibid.: 25).

- Jesse Norman, MP, in his report in *The Sunday Times* (2011) proposed an increase in music provision in schools, the promotion of choirs and orchestras and suggested that music is 'not a wheeze; it is part of the wiring'.

Summary

Through the activities presented to children in their early years, children are able to assimilate information from their environment, their peers, their family members and other older children and adults. They are able to role-play, explore and interact with their world. Providing a wide range of experiences nourishes children's brains and enables them to make the connections necessary for future development. Music may enhance a child's development even prior to birth.

Pre-school music is not just a good idea; the benefits to be derived are extensive. Music provides a medium that is fun, engaging, relaxing and creative and one that may create connections that enable future language skills to flourish. As you will learn in the next chapter, many of the skills acquired through musical activities are almost synonymous with the skills required for literacy. The participation in pre-school music requires no prior knowledge or skill. A child need only be present at a music session in order to gain from the experience. Children are naturally inquisitive and even the most reticent of children will usually participate and certainly benefit in some way. Music provides a non-threatening medium through which much experience can be gained.

In the school environment music may continue to support many areas of learning, including language and particularly literacy.

Something to think about

- How do you think that musical activities may help to promote literacy skills? What songs do you know that you could use with children?

- Does background music help children to focus or is it distracting?

- For each activity presented so far, in addition to the particular skills stated, think about other skills that may be developed through the activity.

- As in several of the activities in this chapter, set your own words to familiar tunes to put across your own messages or to complement a current theme.

Something to read

Harrop, B. and Sanderson, A. (1994) *Okki-tokki-unga: Action Songs for Children*. London: A. and C. Black.

Hart, J. (1983) *Sing a Song of Sixpence! The Best Song Book Ever*. London: Victor Gollancz Ltd.

Matterson, E. (compiled by) (1991) *This Little Puffin*. London: Penguin Books Ltd. An excellent source of rhymes, songs and games for children.

Umansky, K. (1996) *Three Singing Pigs: Making Music with Traditional Stories*. London: A. and C. Black.

Useful websites

The publication *Learning Through Play in the Early Years* compiled by the Early Years Interboard Panel in Northern Ireland contains many ideas for musical activities. This may be accessed online at: http://www.nicurriculum.org.uk/docs/foundation_stage/learning_through_play_ey.pdf

http://www.babyplus.com – prenatal education system

http://www.drakemusicscotland.org – information on 'Figurenotes', a note reading system using colour and shape

http://www.guidinguk.freeservers.com – campfire songs

http://www.kididdles.com – songs for young children

http://www.mamalisa.com – songs from around the world

http://www.piano4kids.com and www.noteimals.com – the 'animal notes' method of teaching musical note reading to children

http://www.singandsign.com – communication for babies

http://www.singup.org – resources for teachers in England

http://www.soundbeam.co.uk – a system for generating sound through movement

http://www.soundsandsymbols.co.uk – the literacy-through-music programme based on this book

http://www.youthmusic.org.uk – information about musical events and programmes in the UK

2

Investigating literacy development

This chapter covers

- Defining literacy

- What is reading?

- What is writing?

- Reading readiness: ready to read?

- What skills do children need before they learn to read?

- Literacy and music in the early years curriculum

- How do children learn to read?

- Phonics first

- Reading strategies employed since the 1970s

- Popular current reading schemes

- How do children learn to write?

Defining literacy

A widely accepted definition of literacy is the ability to read and write. Described as being illiterate are those who have had no formal education and are unable to read and write. There are very few people who may be termed completely illiterate in the Western world, as most can read or write to some extent. The NLT includes listening and speaking in its definition. The Kansas Standards (USA) also include '**viewing**', referring to visual discrimination.

Literacy may be investigated through:

Listening   Hearing and interpreting sounds

Composition   Exploration of sounds (words) and putting these together in a
                   sequence (speaking and writing)

Movement   Communication through and in response to movement

Speaking   Making vocal sounds

Text   Production of and interpretation of text.

You may recognise that music and literacy can be investigated through the same activities. Indeed they have many areas of commonality.

What is reading?

Reading may take several definitions. We say that we can 'read' an expression in a face; this infers that we are able to understand what a person is feeling. Similarly, it is possible to 'read' a situation. Another use of the term 'reading' is the decoding of symbols. This alone does not imply comprehension or a feel for the text. Although decoding skills are vital to the ability to read, it is comprehension that breathes life into text.

In music, too, children learn to interpret symbols. When children first begin to read music they may be introduced to symbols to represent times when the instrument or sound should be played. The graphic notation illustrated in Chapter 1 provides an example. Graphic notation offers a simplified version of reading musical notation. However, there is no simplified version of text on which children can practise learning to read. Simple, graphic, musical notation can, however, help in the development of sound–symbol correspondence by introducing the concept that sounds can be represented by symbols.

What is writing?

The Concise Oxford Dictionary defines writing as 'a group or sequence of letters or symbols' (Allen, 1990: 417). Writing is used for the conveyance and keeping of records and may or may not be permanent. The ability to write adds a dimension to communication; it facilitates the sending of messages or the recording of thoughts and ideas. Handwriting refers to the physical skill of scribing words onto a page. I am currently writing this book but I am not handwriting, I am generating the text from my head and scribing it via a keyboard into my PC.

Reading readiness: ready to read?

Most people would suggest that we become literate at school but exactly how this happens is a complex process. The DFE believes (DFE, 2012a) that children are ready to begin a programme of systematic synthetic **phonics** work by the age of five. The term 'phonics' refers to a method of teaching reading by correlating sounds with letters or groups of letters in the alphabet. The EYFS framework offers guidance to build the skills and knowledge required by children up to this stage.

A report published by Graham Allen, MP (Allen, 2011: 1) recommended regular assessment of pre-school children and promoted the idea of 'school readiness'. It supported the provision of early **intervention** schemes for children from disadvantaged backgrounds. The report suggests that success or failure in early childhood has 'profound economic consequences; socially and emotionally capable people are more productive, better educated, tax-paying citizens helping our nation to compete in the global economy and make fewer demands on public expenditure' (Allen, 2011: 1).

There is a general assumption that when a child is ready to go to school then they should be ready to learn to read. Should children be ready to learn to read when they start school? The concept of 'school readiness' is discussed by Cassidy (2010). What are the preparations made for entry to compulsory mainstream schooling? Pre-school education is not compulsory, so children arrive at school with differing experiences.

There is much debate and research relating to the question of when children might be ready to learn to read. Doman proposes that it is possible for a child to begin to learn to read at the age of only 10 months but that it would generally be best to begin learning from the age of two years. He believes that the child under the age of five years has a 'monumental desire to learn' (Doman, 1988: 105).

The extent to which parents teach their children to read or expose them to print such as reading stories to them, encouraging word recognition, teaching shapes, letters and patterns varies greatly. It must also be borne in mind that children themselves vary and may be receptive or have a desire to interpret print at different ages.

Heald and Eustice believe that it is never too soon to start sharing books with your child and that children will learn to read when they are ready. They suggest that:

> a child needs to learn about the way language works [...] and must be able to listen and speak confidently and competently before being expected to understand the written forms of language. (Heald and Eustice, 1988: 8)

Thomas (1997) reports that disciples of Rudolf Steiner believe that children are not ready to learn to read until they are six years of age as it is not believed that they are ready for abstract things. She also points to the fact that in Holland, Sweden and Germany, formal schooling starts at the age of seven years without any evident disadvantage. The children do, however, sing songs, act out poems and have stories read to them. Thus the younger children are learning about language – a precursor to learning to read.

What skills do children need before they learn to read?

The concept of pre-reading skills supposes that there is a stage at which one moves from non-reader to reader. This does not in fact appear to be the case as the ability to read increases as more and more is learned about reading. This process may begin from when a book is first read to a child.

From research that I have gathered I would suggest that in order for children to develop the skills required for reading the following points are important.

Children should possess a good facility with language

They need to:

- possess a good command of oral language (Van der Gaag, 1999)

In order to become literate it is important for children to develop good speaking and listening skills. From the first months of life, children's experiences with oral language begin to build the foundations for later reading success. The extent of oral language is highly correlated with later reading proficiency, and Van der Gaag (1999, quoted from the NLT website) found that:

> A high proportion of children (41–75 per cent) with identified speech and language difficulties in their pre-school years go on to have difficulties with reading skills during their school years.

Children who develop a good command of language early have a head start on those who don't. A review by the Expert Panel (DFE, 2011a) suggested that a feature of the new English curriculum for 2014 in England should be oral skills.

Reciting rhymes with children encourages them to listen carefully and to echo back the words that they hear. Using different voices, for example pretending to be a mouse and speaking in a squeaky voice or being a lion with a roaring voice and encouraging children to do the same, helps children to practise making sounds and to appreciate when using different tones, volumes and pitches is appropriate. The early years are the perfect time for this learning. The tune for Activity 2.1 may be used for the lyrics in Activity 2.2 with a slight change in rhythm to match the syllables.

 Activity 2.1   What Does a Mouse Say?

What does a mouse say?

Hey, hey, can anybody play?

What does a mouse say?

Eek, eek, all day long.

Lyrics: M. Kay

It is important to help children to recognise and make sounds through imitation. Encourage children to use different voices by suggesting other creatures, for example a cat, dog, cow, owl or pigeon. Communication involves more than verbal language; facial and body signs also play a role. To reinforce communication skills, add signs, such as those from the British Sign Language (BSL). Using body language and hand signs supports communication; it does not detract from or hinder language development.

- appreciate and be aware of their environment (Smith, 1978) – without a vocabulary to describe their environment children would be unable to relate the written word to their surroundings

- understand language (Heald and Eustice, 1988) – children need to be able to comprehend and respond to language. They will need to learn that written language differs from spoken language. Children must understand the patterns and rhythms in language and become familiar with its structure.

Children need to possess knowledge about text

They need to:

- appreciate that text has meaning and that text has a purpose (Meek, 1982) – it imparts knowledge/feelings and can entertain. Reading rhymes and songs with children also helps them to gain pleasure from the interpretation of text and to assimilate bibliographic knowledge

- assimilate some bibliographic knowledge (Adams, 1990) – in order to know how to read a book, it is necessary to know the direction of the print. It is also necessary to know where a book begins and how a book is compiled.

Children need to have motivation to decode text (Moyle, 1968)

If a person has an enquiring mind this will aid the process of reading. Children often enjoy behaving like readers long before they can read.

Children should possess a variety of skills related to sound

They need to:

- develop an appreciation of rhythm – this helps children to detect syllables, appreciate language structure and fluency (Holliman et al., 2010)

- have a knowledge of rhyme (Goswami, 1997) – this helps the later matching of letters, **blends** and word patterns. Children need to be able to detect similarities and differences in sounds

- be able to internalise sounds – it is important to be able to 'hold' a sound in your head. This helps the learning of sound–symbol correspondence and aids in the ability to know how a word sounds

- be able to match sounds, first to each other for identification and then to their respective alphabetic symbols. This enables children to become accomplished at sound–symbol correspondence – matching **phonemes** to their respective **graphemes**

- be able to detect differences between sounds – this ability is termed **auditory discrimination**

- develop phonological awareness – the ability to detect and manipulate the sounds in words at three levels of sound structure: syllabic, intra-syllabic and phonemic (Kozminsky and Kozminsky, 1995).

Children need to possess skills of visual discrimination

Children need to be able to recognise shape in order to identify letters and words. Children will ultimately need to be able to match letter patterns. They must learn that sounds can be represented by shapes.

Children need to develop a good memory

The ability to recall facts and experiences is very important to learning as we use memory as a foundation on which to build in order to create new ideas and experiences. Memory can be aided by the provision of links – music can provide such linkage as a tune may be able to jog one's memory of the accompanying lyrics.

It is apparent that many of the requirements for reading are related to sound. The ability to identify sounds and match them to their corresponding alphabetic characters is imperative to the initial reading process and something that it is possible to introduce to young children through music. Children can be shown an alphabet book and sing the alphabet to the tune of Twinkle Twinkle Little Star. This will help them to learn letter names and to match them to their corresponding symbols. Initially, learning the letter sounds is most important. A song to assist with this is What Does This Letter Say?

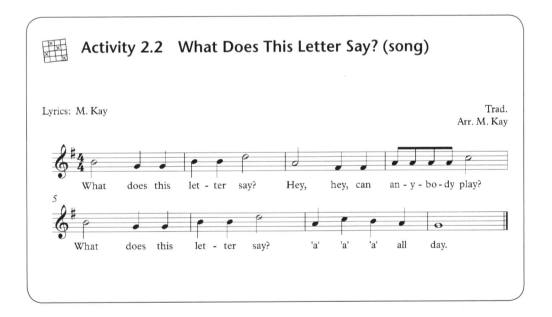

Literacy and music in the early years curriculum

In response to a study by the Basic Skills Agency that showed the crippling effects of illiteracy on physical and mental health in 1996, the School Curriculum Assessment Authority (SCAA) drew up a skills checklist for assessing reception pupils based on the *Desirable Outcomes* booklet. The SCAA checklist (Sainsbury, 1997) for assessing pupils on entry to school made explicit links between the requirements for English in the NC and music.

In 1997, SCAA also produced a document *Music and the Use of Language*, stating that it was 'a requirement of the Music Order for all teachers to consider ways of developing children's use of language' (p.1). The document draws attention to the relationship between language and music at KS One and Two and illustrates how they can be developed together. In Scotland, the Curriculum for Excellence (CfE) introduced in 2011, for all children aged 3–11 years, expects literacy and numeracy to be the responsibility of all teachers across the curriculum. It also encourages links between all curriculum areas. This helps pupils to realise how their skills in one area are transferable to others.

Since 1997, there have been initiatives linking music and literacy such as those by Youth Music and Book Start. Information on these can be found at the end of this chapter. As part of the government's Sure Start services there was also Music Start, but this was discontinued in 2008. Singing songs helps children to appreciate sequence and aids the building of vocabulary. Pointing to words of a song whilst children sing along helps them relate sounds to symbols and helps fluency of reading. Singing has additional benefits such as reducing stress, boosting the immune system and enhancing mood.

The Early Years Foundation Stage (DCSF, 2008) made reference to using stories, songs and rhymes in its framework in the communication, language and literacy area.

The EYFS framework (DFE, 2012a) proposes the use of phonic knowledge in literacy learning. It expresses the following goals related specifically to literacy:

Communication and language early learning goals

Listening and attention: children listen attentively in a range of situations. They listen to stories, accurately anticipating key events and respond to what they hear with relevant comments, questions or actions. They give their attention to what others say and respond appropriately, while engaged in another activity.

Understanding: children follow instructions involving several ideas or actions. They answer 'how' and 'why' questions about their experiences and in response to stories or events.

Speaking: children express themselves effectively, showing awareness of listeners' needs. They use past, present and future forms accurately when talking about events that have happened or are to happen in the future. They develop their own narratives and explanations by connecting ideas or events. (DFE, 2012a: 7–8)

Literacy early learning goals

Reading: children read and understand simple sentences. They use phonic knowledge to decode regular words and read them aloud accurately. They also read some common irregular words. They demonstrate understanding when talking with others about what they have read.

Writing: children use their phonic knowledge to write words in ways that match their spoken sounds. They also write some irregular common words. They write simple sentences that can be read by themselves and others. Some words are spelt correctly and others are phonetically plausible. (DFE, 2012a: 8–9)

There is no specific mention here of links to music, however, many schools use the phonics resource Letters and Sounds produced in 2007 by the DCFS, founded on the principles of the Rose Review (2006). This resource aims to build children's speaking and listening skills and to develop phonic knowledge and skills. The initial stage – phase one, for nursery/reception children – includes activities of seven types:

- environmental sounds

- instrumental sounds

- body sounds

- rhythm and rhyme

- **alliteration**

- voice sounds

- oral blending and segmenting.

The Letters and Sounds programme focusses on securing word recognition skills to enable children to decode and encode words. It contains many ideas to help children to develop auditory discrimination skills and suggestions for creating opportunities to promote early literacy skills.

The characteristics of effective learning – 'playing and exploring', 'active learning' and 'creating and thinking critically' are listed in the document *Development Matters* (Early Education, 2012: 5). Music can be a form of play, a vehicle for exploration; it certainly promotes active learning and it can ignite the imagination. The activity types from the Letters and Sounds phonics programme can all be delivered through musical activities in order to realise literacy objectives.

Education Scotland advocates use of the Talk to Your Baby resource developed by the NLT. It encourages musical interaction and contains activities for one-to-one and group music activities for babies and young children. The Scottish Arts Council also supports music for young people through its Youth Music initiative.

The use of musical activities to achieve literacy outcomes is not only about performing musically. In order to achieve literacy outcomes, thought must be given as to 'how' the activity can help to do this. For example:

- The reciting of rhymes helps children to recognise sound patterns.

However, for the rhymes to help children with literacy effectively, the children's attention must be drawn to these sound patterns, such that they learn to recognise repeated patterns.

- The use of alliterative rhymes helps children to identify initial letter sounds.

In this case too, attention must be drawn to the repeated sounds so that children learn to recognise the sounds and can then relate them to their alphabetic characters.

- Chanting helps children to maintain a regular rhythm.

Attention should be drawn to the fact that words can have more than one chunk of sound (syllable) and also that we have pauses at the ends of sentences. When chanting, a pause such as that at the end of a sentence is still represented by a beat.

The alliterative chant Five Fat Flies contains each of these forms of language appreciation.

 ### Activity 2.3   Five Fat Flies (rhyme)

Five fat flies flew to the fair,

What did they win when they were there?

Lyrics: M. Kay

When performing this chant encourage the children to recite it too. Tap out the syllables (pat knees), emphasise the initial letter sounds and rhyming line endings. Ask children to repeat the 'f' and 'w' letter sounds. Children could act out being the five flies and flying to the fair. They could think of items that they might win beginning with the sound 'f' or 'w'. They could match the sounds to the letters in an alphabet book. They could 'draw' the letters in the air. Using the printed rhyme children could follow the words as they chant. Reciting chants in this way also helps the development of fluency in oral skills.

Another rhyme that would help to develop oral skills is Mouse, Mouse.

 ### Activity 2.4   Mouse, Mouse (rhyme)

Mouse, mouse, in your house, would you like some lunch?

Here's a piece of lovely cheese, mmm … munch, munch, munch!

Lyrics: M. Kay

Recite the rhyme and place imaginary cheese for the mice to eat. The children run finger mice to the cheese, making excited mice sounds and then eating sounds as they gobble up the cheese. Remember to emphasise initial letter sounds and rhymes; also to reinforce your speech with body language and facial expression.

The DFE recommends the use of music – songs, instruments, rhythm and jingles – as a channel for literacy learning, from birth through to school and beyond. Identifying the source of sound is an important listening skill that can be practised through Activity 2.5.

Activity 2.5   Match Sounds to Their Sources (auditory discrimination activity)

Make a sound with an instrument out of sight and ask the children to identify the instrument. This exercise could be undertaken with other items such as crinkly paper, squeaky toys or recorded sounds.

Memorising sounds and matching them to their source is an early step towards memorising letter sounds. A commonly used activity is that of matching animal sounds to corresponding animal pictures. Such an activity may lead to an investigation of how animals move along and the sounds that they make as they move. Many such sounds are expressed as **onomatopoeias.** Help children to explore the meanings of words such as 'lumber', 'waddle', 'saunter', 'swoop' and 'scamper' through rhymes and songs.

For the song in Activity 2.6, pose the question 'How does an elephant walk?' Discuss words to describe how an elephant might walk.

Activity 2.6   I'm an Elephant (song)

Add more verses such as:

I'm a small, green frog and I hop like this

I'm a tall giraffe and I walk like this

I'm a little mouse and I creep like this

I'm a wise old owl and I fly like this

I'm a crocodile and I snap like this – SNAP, SNAP, SNAP!

Encourage the children to make the animals' sounds, too, as they move along. Discuss which animals move quickly and those that move slowly. Moving to the sounds will help children to remember the words describing them.

The NC for KS One (DFE, 2012c) divides 'English' into three separate areas: Speaking and Listening, Reading and Writing:

- In the *speaking and listening* element children are required to speak clearly, fluently and confidently to different people and to listen, understand and respond to others, also to participate as members of a group and in drama activities.

- In the *reading* element children should be taught word recognition and graphic knowledge, to understand text and to read for information. They are expected to identify sounds and syllables in words, to explore rhyme and *alliteration* [see Activity 2.3].

- In the *writing* element pupils are required to use their knowledge of sound–symbol relationships and phonological patterns.

These references to listening, the discernment of sound patterns and the identification of sounds indicate that the DFE recognises that music has an important part to play in literacy development. The activities detailed so far will contribute to the attainment of the NC requirements.

At the end of Year 1 in primary school (STA, 2012: 7) children are expected to:

- apply phonic knowledge and skill as the prime approach to reading unfamiliar words that are not completely decodable

- read many frequently-encountered words automatically

- read phonically decodable three-syllable words

- read a range of age-appropriate texts fluently

- demonstrate understanding of age-appropriate texts.

An appreciation of the sounds within words such as that which can be gained through musical activities can provide an early foundation for this phonic knowledge.

How do children learn to read?

I believe that children have differing experiences of learning to read and learn at different times and in different ways. Some children can read before they start school. This may be due to parental guidance or help from another child or adult. Children who are inquisitive in this area may start to learn from interpreting environmental print, reading logos or their favourite cereal packet. Children may want to imitate their family's reading activities and be encouraged to join in. Some children can narrate a whole book and appear to be reading when in fact they have memorised the text and are behaving like readers. In this case the desire to read, having a good memory and some bibliographical knowledge are excellent precursors to becoming a good reader. There are currently three main methods that may be used to teach children to learn to read.

Whole word ('whole language' or 'look and say')

In school, teachers may use flash cards to develop a child's sight vocabulary. This method is sometimes called the 'whole word' approach. The words on flash cards often relate to a story that a child knows or to a reading scheme that is shortly to be used. Words may be displayed around the room or the school (this is especially true of nouns, as it is easier for children to learn something that is concrete rather than abstract). To attempt to teach only by this method would necessitate learning more than 200,000 individual words. There is also the question here of whether or not we actually learn to read the word as a whole or whether (as suggested by Adams, 1990) the process of synthesising the letters is so fluent that we do not realise that we are processing the component parts of a word.

Phonics

The most used and maybe also the most controversial method is that of phonics. Phonics is the term used to describe the method of teaching pupils to link a letter or letter pattern to its sound. By learning individual letter sounds such as 'a', 'g', and then blended letter sounds such as 'bl', 'ch', and then strings of letters such as 'ing', 'ight', it is possible to build up full words; this synthesising of sounds is termed **'synthetic phonics'**. This method is strongly encouraged by the DFE. Synthetic phonics helps children to develop **phonemic awareness** – the ability to identify phonemes (the smallest units of sound) in a word.

Analytic phonics is another method of phonics teaching that refers to the learning of a word initially by sight and then taking the word apart such that the sounds and letter patterns in it can be compared to other similar words such as recognising that the beginnings and endings of words may be the same, for example 'spin', 'spade' (beginning) or 'tin' and 'thin' (ending). Ideally, children need to become proficient in manipulating the sounds in words in order to decode and build them.

In 2005 Johnston and Watson reported the results of their seven year Clackmannanshire Study. They examined the effect of synthetic phonics teaching on reading and spelling attainment. They concluded that the synthetic phonics approach was more effective than the analytic phonics approach and that it had a significantly beneficial effect upon reading and spelling ability.

The most obvious benefit (according to Adams, 1990) of phonics is that spelling-sound relations enable independent word learning – words can be sounded out. She believes that awareness that spoken language is composed of words, syllables and phonemes is an extremely important predictor of success in learning to read.

The KS One curriculum details under 'Reading Strategies' that pupils should be taught to:

(a) hear, identify, segment and blend phonemes

(b) sound and name the letters of the alphabet

(c) identify syllables in words

(d) recognise that the same sounds may have different spellings

[...]

(h) link sound and letter patterns, exploring rhyme, alliteration and other sound patterns. (DFE, 2012c: 4)

It is clear that auditory discrimination is of vital importance to the process of learning to read. The foundations for many of the targets above can be laid in the pre-school years.

When considering the sounds in words it is important to be cognisant of the three levels of phonological awareness: syllabic, intra-syllabic and phonemic. First, a word may be broken down into syllables (gra-phic); then into its **onsets** and **rimes** (gr-a, ph-ic); and then into phonemes, the smallest unit of sound that enables one word to be distinguished from another (g-r-a-ph-i-c).

'Onset' and '**rime**' are the terms used to describe the phonological (sound) units of a spoken syllable. A syllable can normally be divided into two parts: the onset, the part of the syllable that precedes the vowel in a word that consists of the initial consonant or consonant blend; and the rime, which consists of the vowel and any final consonants. In the word 'stripe', 'str' is the onset and 'ipe' is the rime. Words that share the same rime will also rhyme, but the spelling will be constant and not vary as it does with rhyme. For example, 'rain', 'rein' and 'reign' sound the same and therefore rhyme but they have different rimes – 'ain', 'ein' and 'eign'. 'Rain', 'pain' and 'plain' all rhyme and have the same rimes.

Without the ability to detect the different sounds in words it becomes very difficult to divide a word into its component parts and subsequently decode it. Music is an ideal medium through which listening skills and auditory discrimination skills can be developed.

Context

The third method used is that of contextual clues. By comprehension of the text so far and an ability to predict what may follow, an unfamiliar word may be read. Sometimes the text itself offers a sufficient clue or explanation. A major question is whether we want a child to gain an overall gist of a text or to decode every word accurately. This target may vary for different texts and for differing purposes.

Children need to understand sequence and thereby develop the ability to predict. Smith (2004), unlike Adams, believes that reading is a natural process in that children try to make sense of text in the same way as they do of everything else in their world. Smith argues that children arrive at text with prior knowledge that they apply to reading, such as what to expect from illustrations, the type of publication and contextual cues.

I believe that context is very important, to the extent that once we know how to decode text and have a substantial reading vocabulary, we cease to decode each word as we instinctively know what the word will be. This is evident in text such as:

> I konw you wlil be albe to usnraedntd tihs eevn tguohh yuo cnonat raed ecah wrod.

In this sentence, the first and last letters of each word are in the place that we would expect them to be in. All the correct letters are present and the length of the words are the same, too. We use all this knowledge to reconstruct the correct words. We use this knowledge to create the correct word from the letters given, which we can in fact do amazingly quickly.

Similarly, if vowels are omitted it is still possible to read words. Try to read this sentence:

> I hp tht y wll b ble t rd ths.

However, it is only possible to do this if the words are in context. For example, the letters 'rd' could be red, road, read, rod, rid or others. This suggests that we do not only rely on the letters but use our knowledge of context, too. When reading this text we would put in the relevant vowels, 'internalising' as we read it and we do not in fact read what is written but what we expect to be written.

A study by Bryant and Bradley in 1980 (in Goswami and Bryant, 1990) showed that children find nonsense words more difficult to read than those with which they can make analogies. This difficulty in reading nonsense words illustrates that children use contextual clues when reading. When there is no sense to a word then all that it is possible to do is use phonological knowledge to read it. When reading text, children and adults alike align what they think that the word will be with a word in their vocabulary that also matches the context of the sentence.

An ability to apply all three learning methods would seem to give a child the greatest chance of success. Proficient readers are likely to use all three. However, there is research to show that teaching the three methods simultaneously would be detrimental.

The Clackmannanshire study (Johnston and Watson, 2005) found that teaching a mixture of methods did not work well as it could be confusing to present pupils with different approaches. Goddard (2002: 114) states that, 'when a child is experiencing difficulties, it is often tempting to try to provide maximum stimulation and support'. A study by Kavale and Mattson (1983) in Goddard (2002) suggested that too many types of simultaneous interventions may cause overload. The brain can only take in a certain amount of information and then needs time to absorb and integrate this.

An evidence paper details support for phonics teaching and advises that 'a single approach is more effective than mixing and matching different schemes' (DFE, 2011b: 6). It expresses the necessity of being able to decode words before moving on to develop fluency and comprehension.

Phonics first

I would suggest that synthetic phonics is an excellent way to start, with whole word and context being used as supporting strategies as decoding skills develop. I also believe that it is imperative that children are taught to spell correctly from the beginning. If children are allowed to misspell words then these erroneous initial spelling attempts become ingrained and are very difficult to correct later. In the 1970s, children were often encouraged to write freely without worrying about correct spelling, which it was believed by some could be corrected later. I do not advocate this at all and believe that there is no sense in having to re-learn what could have been learned correctly at the beginning.

Starting with phonics is also advocated in the USA. A report by Learning Point Associates (2004: 1) states that, incorporated into the No Child Left Behind Act 2001 in the USA are five areas identified by the National Reading Panel Report (National Institute of Child Health and Development, 2000) as essential components to effective reading instruction, these being:

- phonemic awareness

- phonics

- fluency

- vocabulary

- comprehension.

The Learning Point Associates Report (2004: 39) describes 'phonemic awareness' and 'phonics' as 'foundational components' that 'will receive less emphasis as students gain competence as readers'. This suggests that phonics provides a basis upon which further skills can be built. I believe that this is precisely the case and that early participation in musical activities can help to establish such a basis.

Reading methods employed since the 1970s

Until the 1970s, phonics was used for teaching reading in British schools. Thereafter this method was discarded for the new 'look, say' (whole word) method and the use of context to identify words. The reason for this was that there is an argument that not all words can be spelled phonetically and that there are many anomalies in the English language. Where children are taught only to spell phonetically their spelling of course falls short of adequate. Learning to read was taught by 'flash cards'. Children learned to recognise individual words and gradually built up a reading vocabulary.

In the 1980s, the Real Book approach was used – reading books with children and gaining an overall understanding of how books work before learning individual words. The reasoning for this method was to engender an interest in books and reading by presenting exciting text. By the 1990s, standards in reading were falling and there was a need for reform. There began to be a return to phonics.

The National Literacy Project (NLP) 1996, which was set up in 15 local authorities, advocated the systematic and challenging teaching of phonics, spelling and vocabulary at KS One and Two. There was an emphasis on the spoken word and use of music. Listening skills were regarded as important in the development of phonological and phonemic awareness in the early stages.

There was a substantial increase in reading scores between 1998 and 2000 that, according to the National Literacy Strategy (2001) published by the Department for Education and Employment (**DfEE**), was as a result of more systematic and better structured teaching of reading. The Literacy Hour was introduced in 1996–99. It included whole class reading or writing, whole class word and sentence level work, including phonics and spelling and group activities. A report published in 2004 by the Centre for the Economics of Education found a positive and significant effect resulting from the implementation of the literacy hour (Machin and McNally, 2004).

In 1998, teachers were encouraged to use the Searchlight Model – using phonics, whole word recognition, grammatical knowledge and contextual clues to teach children to read.

The Every Child a Reader scheme backed by the UK government and started in 2005 had significant success. It aimed to ensure that every child achieved age-related expectations at the end of KS One. It delivered intensive one-to-one tuition for children who were struggling. It incorporated Reading Recovery, which was developed in 1993 to help those who were not reaching the expected levels of literacy attainment. By 2012, due to government spending cuts, schools were finding it difficult to maintain this provision.

A report by Torgerson et al. (2006), commissioned by the Department for Education and Skills (**DfES**), recommended systematic phonics instruction as a teaching strategy. A review by Jim Rose, also in 2006, recommended high quality, systematic phonic work. He proposed that phonic work for young children should be multi-sensory. By 2007, phonics was back in favour. In 2007–08, schools were obliged to follow the amended curriculum arising from the Rose Review. Despite the recommendations from the Rose Review, Coldwell et al. (2011) found that only 27 per cent of schools participating in their evaluation were delivering a dedicated phonics programme as the prime approach to reading.

Including the evidence from the Clackmannanshire Study (Johnston and Watson, 2005), support for phonics was increasing. In the summer of 2011, the British government conducted trials of 'phonics screening tests' for children at the end of their first year in primary school. This was undertaken with a view to identifying children who needed to improve their phonic decoding skills. The tests conducted were of four to nine minutes' duration and consisted of reading a list of 20 real and 20 pseudo-words. The results of the tests revealed that only 32 per cent of 6 year olds reached the expected level of phonic decoding to an age-appropriate standard. Actual screening began in June 2012.

Although I am clearly a proponent of phonics, I have one caveat. I am not convinced of the value of teaching children to read nonsense words on a regular basis. In order to prepare children for testing, it is possible that they may become over-focused on 'sounding out' words rather than reading to gain meaning from text. This would seem to me to negate the purpose of reading if there was no meaning to be gained and would serve the needs of the test setter rather than the child.

Popular current reading schemes

One popular scheme that promotes the learning of letter sounds is *Letterland* (Carlisle and Wendon, 1992). This scheme uses alliteration and visual stimulus. For example, the letter 'C' is named Clever Cat and the letter itself is illustrated as a cat. 'W' is 'Wicked Water Witch' and the letter is illustrated with a picture of a witch within it. The bold pictures and alliterative names make the letters easy to remember. Words with the same initial letter sound and associated pictures are displayed. The vowel sounds are highlighted.

Once letter sounds are learned, the sounds and letters can be joined together, for example c-a-t for cat. This method may be further developed to include blends and **digraphs**, also letter strings, for example 'ight', 'ing', and 'tion'.

This method is also advocated by Cowling and Cowling (1993), who developed a very successful reading programme *Toe By Toe*, with an emphasis on sound–symbol correspondence. The programme is designed to be used on a one-to-one basis by non-professionals and as such has been used mainly to support other programmes.

The Phonics Handbook (Lloyd, 1992) identifies 42 phonemes (The British Received Pronunciation in *Letters and Sounds* recognises 44) and puts actions to these sounds; the actions create a fun and kinaesthetic learning opportunity. This system has been used extensively by schools and is very popular.

The *Letters and Sounds* phonics programme was recommended by the DCSF in light of the Rose Review and was used by schools from 2007. In the notes for guidance (DCSF, 2007: 14), advice is given to the effect that: 'The best route for children to become fluent and independent readers lies in securing phonics as the prime approach to decoding unfamiliar words.'

How do children learn to write?

The National Literacy Strategy (introduced by the DfEE in 1998, updated in 2002) suggested that young children learn to write through:

- developing oral language (pp. 48–59)

- reading with an adult individually and/or in a group (pp. 62–3)

- playing games which help them to hear sounds in words and form the letters that represent them (pp. 60–1 and 66–7)

- playing and experimenting with writing and watching others write (pp. 64–5).

A child's first attempts at writing may consist of the making of marks on paper, 'mark making'. By examining the difference between a young child's early attempts at drawing and writing, it can be seen that the writing will often consist of lines or squiggles that a drawing does not. Children often want to imitate their parents' writing of shopping lists, notes or letters and will behave like writers. They learn that text has meaning and that their thoughts and words can be recorded on paper.

When learning to write, children need to know the sounds, names and form of the letters of the alphabet. The publication *Letters and Sounds* (DCSF, 2007: 16) suggests that learning a letter comprises:

- distinguishing the shape of the letter from other letter shapes

- recognising and articulating a sound (phoneme) associated with the letter shape

- recalling the shape of the letter with the correct movement, orientation and relationship to other letters

- naming the letter

- being able to recall and recognise the shape of a letter from its name.

In pre-school and primary school, children are taught sound–symbol correspondence and practise copying letter shapes and subsequently words. Children may learn to write their names in the sky and practise making shapes to music.

 Idea

Teach children the names of geometric and letter shapes. Write the shapes in the air using scarves or ribbons; write shapes, lines and circles in flour, sand and gloop. Help children to learn to recognise their own name in writing. Help children to learn how to place the letters in their name in the correct order – use plastic or wooden letters. Encourage children to write to music – large, slow circles to slow music and fast squiggly lines to fast music.

A song to help with the practise of writing skills is Can You Make a Circle? Perform the actions as suggested by the lyrics. Start with large movements and progress to smaller ones.

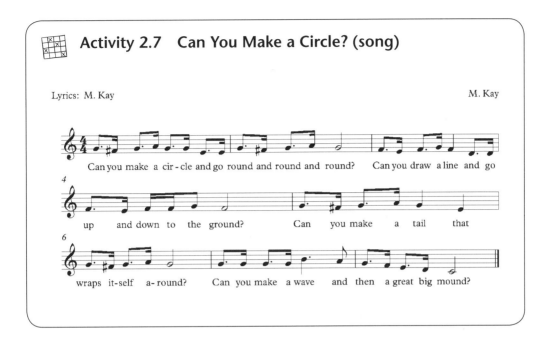

The physical skill of handwriting requires fine motor control. Fine motor skills can be practised through the manipulation of small toys such as construction bricks/pieces, tools, painting, drawing, threading, fastening buttons, opening and closing zips, making puzzles and anything else that requires precise hand and finger movements. Learning to control and play instruments also assists in fine motor development. Plucking strings, tapping claves, shaking maracas, beating drums, scraping a guiro, rolling a cabasa or clicking castanets all help to hone hand manipulation skills.

In addition to the fine motor control required to manipulate a writing implement, children also need to be able to match patterns visually. They must also have an awareness of orientation on a page and an awareness of how words are spaced. They will need to be able to place letters in the appropriate place between lines on paper. An activity that will help to accomplish these skills is Building Bricks. Using four rectangular building bricks, sing or recite the rhyme and build structures as determined by the lyrics.

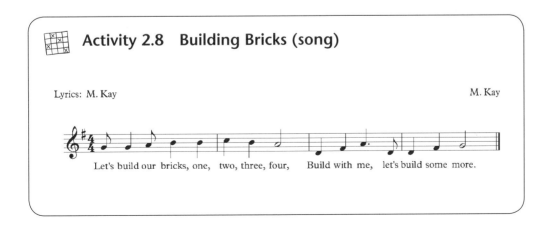

You can build a wall, make an arrow, pillars, two columns, a tower, form a square or any other arrangement from your imagination. Use bricks of different colours and encourage the children to place their bricks in the same order as you. Let the children take turns to choose which construction to make.

This group activity helps to build visual discrimination (viewing) skills and fine motor skills together, in addition to rhyme, rhythm, listening and social skills.

Many young children own computerised games and are introduced to symbols and text through this medium. Fine motor skills are required to manipulate the mouse. Children may also be required to key in text – an early writing (although not handwriting) skill.

Once a child has learned the relationship between spoken and written words, they will be able to write their own words. Possessing a good vocabulary helps children to be prolific writers. In order to write it is necessary to hold an 'internal' dictionary in the head, such that a child knows how words should look when committed to paper. With the fine motor skills necessary, children are then able to begin to construct their own writing.

Children need to understand the purpose of writing; it may be to make a record, to advise, to instruct or to entertain. Written language is different from that which is spoken. The written word is permanent and needs to be more concise and explicit and the writer cannot confirm if necessary, as a speaker could do. As with spoken language, written language becomes increasingly rich and sophisticated. Writers must ensure that their message is clearly conveyed (free from double meaning). Effective communication is achieved by the use of correct **grammar**, **syntax**, choice of vocabulary, language style, tone and punctuation. Being able to construct a piece of writing is a necessary skill for life as it is an important form of communication.

The Latin alphabet we use to record the sounds that we make is not wholly phonetic, unlike Arabic, for example, where one letter represents one sound. (In Arabic, each letter can change shape, depending on its positioning within a word, so this adds greater complexity.) In English, a letter in a word may appear unrelated to its name or sound, for example, the 'x' in 'xylophone'. It may not be sounded at all, such as the 'b' in 'comb' or 'debt'. Some spellings seem to have no sound–symbol correspondence, for example the word 'one'. Writing is maybe more difficult than reading, as when we are reading we can match the sounds to words that we know or something close to them. To initiate the spelling of a word that we have not previously read can be very difficult. Children must learn spelling patterns that they can apply as well as how to spell words with irregular patterns. Learning to write is a continuous process that may begin in infancy and continue throughout life.

Summary

This chapter has outlined what is meant by the term 'literacy' and the skills required for children to become literate. Speaking and listening are prerequisites to reading and writing; music provides a wonderful medium for the practise and development of both.

Many of the skills that are required for literacy development can be promoted through participation in musical activities. The concomitant skills mentioned so far that may be elicited through music for literacy are summarised below in Figure 2.1.

Figure 2.1   Skills Developed through Musical Activities which Contribute to Literacy Competence

Something to think about

- For the children you are working with, choose rhymes or songs specifically to elicit a particular literacy skill. Monitor the progress made.

- Think about the skills required to become literate, consider which ones children may find the most difficult and see if you can find musical activities to help to develop those skills.

- For Activity 2.4, Mouse, Mouse, list as many possible literacy outcomes as you can. Think up a tune to accompany the rhyme.

Something to read

Browne, J. (1991) *Sing Me a Story: Action Songs to Sing and Play*. London: Random Century Group Ltd.

Useful websites

http://www.letters-and-sounds.com – resources to help literacy
http://www.literacytrust.org.uk – information about learning to read

Evidence of analogies between music and literacy

This chapter covers

- Common rhythms: international language and music

- Research supporting links between music and literacy

- The importance of sound to reading

Much of the evidence described in this chapter is from researchers with a science or music background, these being psychologists, neuroscientists and musicians. They have drawn together related strands from music and literacy. As language is implicit within literacy, studies correlating music and language are also noted.

Historically there has been interest in the links between music and language and it has been proposed that they may even have evolved together (Darwin in Brown, 2001; and Burling, 2007). In this case the supposition would be that they have common roots.

Common rhythms: international language and music

Goddard (2002) suggests that the native language and music of an area share a common accent. This is confirmed by Patel (2007), who found that speech rhythm is reflected in the musical rhythm of a language. Similarly, the music of tonal languages is reflected in the use of their instruments. For example, the Thai xylophone has different pitches and **intervals** to European xylophones and this is possibly reflective of the pitches and tones in the language. Sloboda (1989) also makes reference to commonality between a language and its music. Additionally, all languages consist of phonemes and all music consists of notes; these vary according to culture.

Brown (2001), a neurologist, has coined the term 'musilanguage' to describe his hypothesis, building on Darwin's belief that music and language have common ancestry. 'Musilanguage' is a stage of evolution wherefrom music and language have developed. Brown also describes music and language as two forms of auditory communication and suggests that they are **homologous** in that they possess comparative features.

Research supporting links between music and literacy

The emergence of studies investigating the therapeutic benefits of music such as those for **aphasia** – difficulty with or inability to use or understand language – are doing much to support the use of music for promoting language development. As language underpins all learning and forms a basis for later literacy skills, the development of a facility with language is pivotal to later literacy development. Literacy teachers have long acknowledged the importance of rhymes and songs in the promotion of language skills, yet research to support this from a literacy perspective remains sparse.

When I initially set about my investigation in 1996 into the commonalities between music and literacy, I found little material in the UK that specifically sought to link the two elements. This fact was confirmed by Lamb and Gregory (1993: 20), who stated that: 'Studies enquiring into the relationship between musical perception and reading skill are very limited in number.' Hansen et al. (2004: viii) reported similarly that: 'We are aware that little empirical research has been done to validate the causal relationships between music and reading literacy.'

However, there is now a wealth of research evidence, much of which comes from the USA, to advocate that musical activities for early years can have a positive effect on later literacy learning. Most of the research is from a music standpoint. Over the last 20 years the interest in this area has intensified in the USA, Canada and the UK, particularly due to the resurgence of the popularity of phonics in teaching reading and also to the availability of brain imaging techniques, enabling the responses of the brain to be monitored.

Some of the researchers who have drawn correlations between music and literacy or language since 1969 are detailed below.

Kokas

In 1969, Kokas reported improvements in reading in a normal school population in Hungary after introducing the Kodály system of teaching music (based on listening and singing) into the curriculum. It is possible that the focus on listening, reinforced by singing, further reinforcement by hand signals and the use of movement, may well have been contributory factors to the improved reading scores (Kokas, 1969).

The Kodály system of teaching music is one in which concepts are introduced through musical experience, listening, singing and movement. Movement is used to reinforce rhythm. The pentatonic (5-note) scale is taught and hand signals are used to consolidate learning.

McMahon

McMahon (1979) trained young children to discriminate between pairs of 3-note chords. This was found to improve word recognition, reading and general phonic skills, compared with a matched, untrained group.

It seems logical that early training in auditory discrimination would help children when they are listening later to letter sounds and sound patterns in reading, as they will then already be adept at detecting differences in sound.

Douglas and Willatts

Douglas and Willatts (1994) conducted a study on children who were identified as having reading difficulties. They were given a music programme for six months. This was designed to help the children's auditory, visual and motor skills. They used their voices and tuned and untuned percussion instruments to play a variety of games incorporating rhythm and pitch activities. There was frequent change from auditory to visual processes and a combination of both. The findings of this investigation indicated that a link exists between musical ability and reading ability and that the training in music skills led to an improvement in reading.

Douglas and Willatts (ibid.) also reported the findings of an aural awareness test produced by the Music Department of Fife Region. The results of this test showed that an awareness of rhythm was highly correlated with reading and spelling. Combined aural measures (pitch and rhythm) correlated significantly with reading but not with spelling.

Kay

My own research (Kay, 1997: 47) was conducted on parents and carers of pre-school children who were receiving musical activity sessions. The results showed that the sample group were aware of the links between music and literacy and 100 per cent of the respondents believed that musical activities could contribute to successful literacy development.

Moyeda et al.

Moyeda et al. (2006) found that: 'melody and timbre discrimination activities help to stimulate **receptive vocabulary** development'. A receptive vocabulary is that which consists of words that a person understands when reading, watching or listening, this includes the **productive vocabulary**. The productive vocabulary is the vocabulary that is understood and comfortably used in writing and speaking. Moyeda et al. designed a programme of musical activities to promote discrimination of rhythmic and melodic elements and the association of auditory stimuli with visual stimuli and motor activities. The effects on the vocabulary of pre-school children were evaluated. The results showed significant increases in receptive vocabulary.

Wiggins

Wiggins also suggests links between music and reading:

> There are parallel skills in reading and music. A music-integrated literacy environment nurtures auditory and visual discrimination, eye-motor coordination, visual sequential memory, language reception, vocabulary development, phonological and phonemic awareness, and fluency. Simultaneously, musical perception, music score reading, musical memory, song repertoire, and musical performance are enhanced. In the early learning setting, music's engaging nature encourages children to attend during reading activities, invites them to be active listeners, and promotes comprehension and dialogue. (Wiggins, 2007: 62)

Bolduc

Bolduc reviewed literature on the effects of music instruction. He summarised and compared 13 studies examining the relationship between music education and emergent literacy in pre-school children and his findings 'showed the extent to which interdisciplinary programs in music and language can promote basic learning in both subjects, as early as preschool'. He concluded that: 'many authors and researchers claim that musical activities promote the development of three important components that are equally involved in the development of linguistic abilities – auditory perception, **phonological memory** *and* **metacognitive knowledge**' (Bolduc, 2008).

D'Agrosa

D'Agrosa (2008: 7) makes connections between teaching music and teaching reading. She says that listening and speaking are pre-reading skills and ones that can be practised through music. She also suggests that print awareness is a simple way to support the connection between music and reading as the conventions of both are the same, that is, left to right, top to bottom. She proposes that making connections between the two enhances both. D'Agrosa states that:

> Identifying and making oral rhymes is a way that children can demonstrate their phonological awareness. Oral rhymes are an integral part of not only a reading classroom but also a music classroom. (D'Agrosa, 2008)

She also draws connections between syllables and rhythms and demonstrates how vocabulary, fluency and comprehension can be helped by musical activities.

Darrow

Darrow (2008: 32) suggests that 'the magic of music can entice a child to practice various reading-related tasks, often without the child being aware of the learning objective'. She draws attention to the legislation in the USA attempting to facilitate a fully literate nation, the No Child Left Behind Act 2001. In order to implement this, children are screened for possible early reading failure and remediation is begun. Darrow states that nearly one third of children have difficulty learning to read and that no one method of teaching reading appears to be effective.

Darrow discusses cases where music teachers have designed musical activities to teach specific reading skills, for example the work of Kay Roskam, a music therapist. Roskam demonstrated the effectiveness of specifically planned music activities, as they helped learning-disabled children to expand their auditory perception and improved their language skills.

Mizener

Mizener (2008: 11) in the journal *General Music Today*, explains the parallel relationship that exists between music and language and specifically in transmitting and receiving information and says that 'singing and chanting provide practice in rhythm, form, dynamics and mood, which are concepts and skills common to language and music'.

This particular volume of the publication is dedicated to the overlap of skills used in both music and literacy and the following list of music concepts and their reading labels is provided by Melissa Berke, Chair, Society for General Music. She says that: 'music teaches reading!' (Berke, 2008: 5).

Reading Concepts	Music Concepts
Letter recognition	Note recognition
Sound–symbol association	Sound–symbol association
Syllabification	Performing rhythm patterns
Vocabulary	Vocabulary
Rhyming	Rhyming lyrics
Parts of speech	Elements of music
Sentence structure	Phrase structure
Punctuation	Articulation
Story writing	Composition
Comprehension	Aural analysis
Silent reading	Audiation
Fluency	Fluency

The reference of Mizener to language would appear to assume that literacy is dependent on language, since the articles are proposing parallels between music and literacy. This is indeed the case if we wish to incorporate comprehension and meaning into the definition of literacy.

To be literate is to be able to use language and to read and write it. The ability to become literate assumes that we have a facility with language. It is possible to suggest that music itself is a language, as does Longfellow:

> Music is the universal language of mankind. (Longfellow, 1835: 4)

As the commonalities between music and literacy are being identified by many researchers, it can be seen that the various aspects exposed are being stated repeatedly.

Gardner

Gardner is the founder of the concept of 'multiple intelligences'. He identified seven types of intelligence and suggested that there may be more. These can be used to identify a person's possible preferred learning style. A person having strengths in one area could use this area to strengthen the others. He suggests that most of us are predominantly strong in three of his identified intelligence types.

Gardner (1985) believes that musical intelligence runs in an almost structural parallel to linguistic intelligence. Language skills tend to be high in people whose base intelligence (as defined by Gardner) is musical. They are likely to use songs or rhythms to learn. They would be sensitive to rhythm, pitch, **metre**, tone, melody or timbre.

Stansell

Stansell (2005) approaches the correlations between music and language from a language perspective and describes them as 'supportive sisters' and 'natural partners'. In his article 'The use of music for learning languages', he explores the role of music in the learning of language and the commonalities between each. Stansell identifies the following in his introduction as being required in both music and language and suggests that they should be learned together:

- melodic recognition

- contour processing

- timbre discrimination

- rhythm

- tonality

- prediction and

- perception of the sight, sound and form of symbols in context.

He also suggests bringing music therapists into the language classroom in order to integrate music into the language curriculum.

Jordan-DeCarbo

Jordan-DeCarbo (2006) in the journal *Perspectives*, reports the results of a study that established a connection between active involvement with age-appropriate music activities and cognitive development. This would concur with Altenmüller et al. (2006), who suggested that music trains the brain. In particular, Jordan-DeCarbo noted significant gains in six out of eight linguistic tests over the **control group**. This study supported a previous study by Galliford in 2003 confirming that musical exposure in the home and at pre-school had a significant association with both linguistic and non-linguistic skills. This adds further evidence to the positive influence that music can have on the linguistic and other skills of young children.

Patel

Patel (2007) writes of the relationship between 'music, language and the brain' in his book of the same title. He suggests that musicians have more grey matter than non-musicians. Patel's investigation is from a scientific viewpoint and is explored further in Chapter 4.

Taylor and Clark

Research from Taylor and Clark (2007) explored the impact of musical activities on the development of pre-school-aged children over a three-year period in North

Tyneside and Great Yarmouth. One aim of the project was to see if literacy skills of pre-school-age children were improved because of music-making activities.

The findings of the project were that regular, structured, active and creative weekly or biweekly musical activity sessions support development in communication and language skills and understanding, particularly in:

- increasing the amount and quality of speech developed through singing activities

- increased vocabulary

- development of understanding of rhyming through singing

- increased ability to listen and respond to spoken instructions in connection with a musical activity

- learning how conversation works through 'call and response' activities

- development of greater control of their voices through learning to pitch notes – high and low – and pitch match (sing in tune)

- increased ability to tell their own stories through creating their own songs (Taylor and Clark, 2007: 40).

Sacks

The neurologist Oliver Sacks (2008) confirms that we are the only musical species. He states that children spontaneously move to the propulsive effect of musical rhythm. In his book *Musicophilia*, Sacks discusses, amongst his treasury, **amusia**, the inability to recognise music or reproduce it and aphasia, the inability to use or understand language. He draws parallels between the two by demonstrating how aphasia may be overcome through the use of music.

Sacks describes the cacophony heard by an **amusic** when listening to music, this is a far cry from the sweet melodies being enjoyed by a person without this ailment. As the person with amusia will however hear the same sounds being spoken as anyone else, then there must be a difference in the reception of these sounds by the brain. As music and speech are both sounds, the brain must have some way of deciding how to process each separately. As suggested by Sammler (2010), it is possible that the sounds are received together and then processed separately. This is certainly an interesting area for further research.

For most people, many language functions are located in the left hemisphere of the brain. Hence the development of aphasia is linked to damage in this side of the brain. People who are left-handed are more likely to have language areas in both sides of the brain and so may develop aphasia from damage to either side of the brain.

Piro and Ortiz

Piro and Ortiz (2009) examined the effect of piano lessons on vocabulary and verbal sequencing skills – two major components of literacy development – of primary children. They investigated children who had received instruction on piano for three consecutive years in one school and children from another school who received no formal musical training on any instrument. The results showed that the group that had received musical training scored significantly better on vocabulary and verbal sequencing than their non-musical counterparts.

Kraus et al.

Kraus and Chandrasekaran (2010) reviewed research which suggested that children who have received musical training have a better vocabulary and reading ability than those who have not had such training, also that the neural connections made whilst undertaking musical training tones the brain making it able to use these connections for other aspects of communication. Musicians are better at processing speech whilst there is background noise than non-musicians and children with learning disorders have most difficulty hearing speech when there is background noise.

Kraus et al. (in Strait et al. 2011) demonstrated how auditory working memory and musical aptitude are intrinsically related to reading ability. They found that musical experience boosts sensitivity to sound patterns; hence it may be useful to literacy learning.

The importance of sound to reading

Such was the emphasis placed by the British government in 2012 on the importance of sound to reading, that phonics screening was delivered to 600,000 Year 1 pupils in England. Children who did not reach the expected standard in phonic decoding (over 235,000) were to receive additional intervention and be considered for a retake of the phonics screening check a year later.

The reversion to the emphasis on phonics teaching suggests that educationalists believe that it is increasingly important for children to be able to differentiate sounds and identify the sound components of words. The role of pre-school and school music should therefore assign significant attention to the honing of children's auditory awareness and processing in an effort to support literacy.

In order to learn any language it is important to be able to process the sounds that we hear. This auditory processing requires us to assimilate several types of information (Goddard, 2002: 108): vibration, sound, rhythm, timing and orientation (hearing what is around and behind us). Goddard (ibid.: 108) suggests that music can be used to improve auditory processing. To facilitate the development of auditory awareness, activities such as the following should be undertaken by children:

- sounding out the syllables in words

- singing songs and rhymes

- moving to music and

- slowing down songs to emphasise speech sounds.

Emphasising the sounds in words through song helps children to identify all parts of a word. Children with spelling difficulties often miss out parts of a word when they try to write it down. Tapping or clapping and then sounding out the syllables in a word helps to identify individual parts of a word. Sounding out words slowly also gives a child more time to consider the individual sounds within it and their respective order.

It is easy to use instruments or make body sounds to assist in the stressing of syllables in words. When undertaking the Activity 3.1, help the children to identify the syllables correctly by repeating their responses slowly and enunciating the syllables carefully.

 Activity 3.1   Syllables

Ask the children to tap out the syllables of their names or those in the answer to a question such as 'What did you have for breakfast?' Hold a drum and pass a beater to each child in turn. Ensure that the children understand the task required by modelling what you want the children to do. They may require help initially; in this case tap and enunciate the syllables together.

There is much evidence to support the importance of being able to identify rhyme, sounds and pattern. Researchers Goswami and Bryant (1990: 147) state that, 'Children who are sensitive to rhyme eventually do much better at reading.' They believe that a pre-school skill that children bring to reading is the ability to divide a word into its onset and rime and that attending to this ability will have a positive effect on their literacy skills.

Some rhymes have ending words with the same spelling pattern, for example the traditional rhyme Wee Willie Winkie. Highlighting the sound–symbol correspondence to children encourages them to make more analogies for themselves.

 Activity 3.2   Wee Willie Winkie (rhyme)

Wee Willie Winkie ran through the town,

Upstairs and downstairs in his night gown,

Tapping at the windows, crying through the locks,

'Are the children in their beds?' It's past 8 o'clock!

Children are often asked to read solitary words. They need to be able to recognise letter patterns in order to do this. Comparing what is seen to what is already known about letter patterns is to make an **analogy** between the two. Children need to employ phonic skills and be able to make analogies with words with the same pattern in order to read new words. For example, if a child can already recognise the word 'light' and is able to make analogies, then they will recognise the sound pattern in order to read other words with the same sound ending, for example 'flight' or 'sight'.

Darrow (2008: 32) says that research by Foorman et al. (1997) determined that reading problems occur when children fail to be able to decode a single word. They found that decoding is dependent on sensitivity to the sound structure of language. Children must be able to identify letter sounds and the component sounds in words. Darrow states that: 'there is a growing body of literature that supports specific music experiences and activities to teach and practice essential literacy learning components', and says that many of the abilities required for reading can easily be incorporated in and paired with musical experiences. She believes that music and reading are 'a natural fit' (Darrow, 2008: 33).

Research by Adams (1990) showed that an awareness of syllables and phonemes is an extremely important predictor of success in learning to read. In response to the debate in the USA over phonics versus whole language, Adams produced a report that evaluated alternative methods of learning to read. From the research involved, she proposed that: 'Programs that include some explicit, systematic phonic instruction tend to produce better word reading skills than those that do not' (Adams, 1990: 93).

Lamb and Gregory (1993) found that the discrimination of musical sounds is related to reading performance but that the influential factor is a specific awareness of pitch changes. Douglas and Willatts (1994) also confirmed a significant correlation between awareness of pitch and reading attainment. An activity I have used with pre-school children to help them to appreciate variations in pitch is Activity 3.3.

 Activity 3.3   Slide Whistle (pitch activity)

Use a slide whistle (I call it my 'wiggle whistle') to make high and low sounds. With children standing, ask them to stretch up their arms and reach up to the sky when the sound is high and to crouch down to touch the floor when the sound is low. Tell the children that when the whistle 'wiggles' (move the slide up and down quickly in the middle) then they are to wiggle, too. The children then have to listen carefully to the changes in pitch and respond accordingly. After the 'wiggle' in the middle, the children need to listen carefully in order to identify whether the change in pitch is up or down. Make sure that you model what you want the children to do.

Kozminsky and Kozminsky extended the findings of Goswami and Bryant and attempted to correlate phonological awareness and reading success. They demonstrated that:

> Phonological awareness development training at a relatively young age (five years) prior to the developmental maturity of the phonological systems, has a sustained effect on reading comprehension skills during the first years of school. (Kozminsky and Kozminsky, 1995: 200)

Of greatest interest to myself was research undertaken by Standley and Hughes (1997), who delivered a 15-week music programme with activities that involved word recognition, children's literature and spontaneous writing. The findings of the study revealed that music programmes improved the reading and writing skills of children and that the programme involving literacy activities also appeared to be more effective in relation to greater phonological awareness. A replication of this study on a larger sample was carried out by Register (2001: 239). She states that: 'Overall results demonstrated that music sessions significantly enhanced the ability to learn prewriting and print concepts' (ibid.).

It would appear that a good phonological awareness correlates positively with reading development and that musical activities can help to develop phonological awareness; hence, musical activities should be able to provide a vehicle for developing a foundation for later reading skills. Further evidence to support this is detailed in a review by Lonie (2010).

The New London Orchestra (NLO) launched a project (2011–13) aiming to increase pupils' literacy skills through music by giving tools and confidence in using musical activities to teachers. They offered workshops to integrate music with literacy teaching. An assessment of the impact of the programme, in which 268 children aged between six and seven years of age took part in 2011, revealed a significant improvement in reading competency compared with a control group (Welch et al., 2011).

Summary

In this chapter research has been cited to support the use of specific musical activities to assist in the development of literacy skills. It should be noted that the development of literacy skills has been a deliberate intention, this is an important consideration. The evidence for the benefits reported may be summarised as shown in Table 3.1.

Table 3.1   Evidence reported of the benefits to literacy skill development derived from the undertaking of specific musical activities

Musical activities	Evidence reported for benefits in
Kodály system	Reading
Auditory discrimination (pairs of 3-note chords)	Word recognition, reading, phonic skills
Rhythm and pitch activities	Reading
Melody and timbre discrimination activities	Receptive vocabulary
Musical activities in general	Auditory discrimination, phonological memory and metacognitive knowledge, vocabulary
Print awareness	Bibliographic knowledge
Identifying and making oral rhymes	Phonological awareness
Rhythms	Syllabification
Singing and chanting – rhythm, form, dynamics and mood	Rhythm, form, dynamics and mood in language
Tones to structure phrases and phrases to compositions	Combining letters to make words and words to form sentences
Adding expression in music by variation of tone or accent by dynamics or tempo	Adding expression in language by patterns of stress or intonation
Visual writing system – sound–symbol correspondence	Visual writing system – sound–symbol correspondence
Appreciation of musical pattern	Appreciation of pattern in language
Recognition of melody	Recognising patterns
Knowledge of structure to enable anticipation and prediction	Knowledge of structure to enable anticipation and prediction

(Continued)

(Continued)

Musical activities	Evidence reported for benefits in
Musical exposure in the home	Significant association with linguistic and non-linguistic skills
Singing	Fluency and quantity of speech and understanding of rhyme
Call and response activities	Conversation
Pitching of notes	Voice control
Creating songs	Storytelling
Musical rhythm	Reflected in speech rhythm
Singing songs and rhymes, moving to music, sounding out syllables and slowing down songs to emphasise speech sounds	Auditory awareness
Rhymes	Reading
Awareness of pitch changes	Reading
Discrimination of musical sounds	Reading
Phonological training – listening games, identifying and creating rhymes	Reading
Movement	Motor skills
Memorising songs and rhymes	Memory

Something to think about

- Think about how you could integrate musical activities into your literacy curriculum.

Something to read

Bolduc, J. and Fleuret, C. (2009) 'Placing music at the centre of literacy instruction', *What Works? Research into Practice, Research Monograph*, No. 19, May, available at: http://www.edu.gov.on.ca/eng/literacynumeracy/inspire/research/whatWorks.html (accessed May 2012). Interesting reading on how musical activities can enhance early literacy development.
General Music Today (2008) 21 (2). This issue of the journal is dedicated to the overlap of skills between music and literacy.

Useful websites

http://www.nlo.co.uk/community_music.html – information on the New London Orchestra's literacy through music project (2011–13)

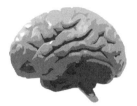

The processing of music and language in the brain

The development of the brain

From the evidence related so far we can see that research suggests that music and literacy have much in common. With current advances in neuroscience and the ability to undertake brain imaging, there is increasing interest in the interrelationship between music and language within the brain.

The nerve cells in the brain (neurons) begin to connect when a child is born. Our brains automatically begin to assimilate the language that we hear. Logically, the greater the exposure to experience, the more connections can be made by the brain. The neurons are connected by junctions that are called **synapses**. The neurons in the brain need to be stimulated to make connections. Neurons form new synapses in response to life experiences. The synapses multiply to make trillions of connections. Most of the synapses form a few months after birth. This network of connections influences the capacity of the brain. The provision of stimulating experiences is therefore essential for maximisation of brain development in the early years. Throughout life, active synapses continue to be strengthened and inactive ones weaken.

The brain grows in spurts. Brain activity is highest in the first three years and neurons that are not stimulated lose their synapses. This process is known as 'synaptic pruning'. Fortunately the brain makes use of the pathways that we do keep and these can be kept active with use.

Another important process in brain development is that of myelination. **Myelin** is an insulating layer of protein and fatty substance that conducts electrical signals. It enables the nerves to transmit impulses between the brain and different parts of the body. Myelination is the formation of a myelin sheath around the brain cells. This sheath then forms a 'highway' for messages. The rate of myelination controls the speed at which each brain function develops. It begins in the primary motor and sensory areas and occurs gradually. It takes 10 or 12 years before general development is completed. This accounts for the reason why children process information more slowly than adults. Their ability to absorb information however is high.

Contrary to synaptic pruning, the process of myelination continues into adulthood. Physical activity increases the production of myelin, thus enabling and securing synapse production. Hence, there is a link between physical activity and brain function.

The many parts of a child's brain mature at different times and have varying 'sensitive periods' when they are dependent on appropriate stimulation. The biggest developments in perception and in the formation of cognitive strategies occur in infancy or early childhood, which is why early stimulation is so vital.

The facility to hear begins early, pre-birth, but matures gradually. Auditory development is the most plastic in pre-natal life; it is malleable throughout pre-school and early primary years, continuing as long as synaptic wiring is being refined. This is an important stage for children to develop musical ability. It is also the time to develop what Howard Gardner (1985) terms 'musical intelligence', the sensitivity to sounds, rhythms, tones and music. The ability to detect sounds in a noisy environment emerges in later childhood.

Sound localisation – the ability to identify the origin of a sound in terms of direction and distance – develops until the age of seven. Much of the main 'wiring' of the brain takes place by this time. By the age of eight years, many of the main human functions are established and the brain has been at its most active.

Visual development emerges late and matures quickly; it is almost at maturation at one year. Visual abilities are highly malleable until the age of two years and then somewhat less so until the age of eight or nine years of age. Babies are born with an already highly developed **vestibular** system, which is responsible for balance and movement.

Children begin using memory in a deliberate fashion as early as three years of age. Children who practise recall are more than likely to develop good memory retention than those who don't. Singing with your baby helps to practise recall and can therefore establish the foundation for a good memory.

For emotional development, the first three years are the most vital. Deprivation in this area during this time can have lifelong effects.

The lobes and functions of the brain

There are four main lobes of the brain – frontal, parietal, occipital and temporal. Each lobe is responsible for a different set of functions.

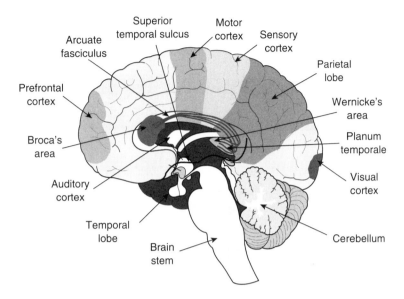

Figure 4.1 Areas of the Brain: Medial View

The frontal lobe controls our emotional responses and speech. The Broca's area is located within the frontal lobe with functions linked to speech production. It helps us to understand the meanings of words and involves word associations. The frontal lobe also helps us to memorise habits and controls motor activities.

The parietal lobe helps us to manipulate objects physically; it helps us to perceive touch and sight. It allows us to integrate senses to enable understanding of concepts.

The occipital lobe is responsible for vision; it may affect our ability to read and write or recognise words.

The temporal lobes at the sides of the head control hearing, memory and some visual perception. These help us to categorise objects. The Wernicke's area, which is responsible for understanding spoken words, is located in this lobe.

With the advent of Magnetic Resonance Imaging (MRI), invented in the 1970s, scientists are now able to detect the brain's response to stimuli and identify active areas of the brain. The MRI machine uses a magnetic field and radio waves and is a non-invasive method of taking detailed pictures of the brain. Prior to this invention, scientists were only able to investigate the brain during postmortems.

When the brain is learning there is heightened activity in the particular area responsible for the subject; many connections are required. Once something is learned it ceases to require such a great level of activity by the brain. The brain is designed to learn and save and then move on to learn the next thing. This supports the argument for lifelong learning.

Left and right brain dominance

Due to the findings of Sperry et al. (in Vinken and Bruyn, 1969: 273–90) in the 1970s, we now know that the two sides of the brain can be responsible for certain functions. The scientists found that by severing the corpus callosum (the membrane connecting the two brain hemispheres) for the treatment of epileptic patients, they were able to determine that the brain depended on a specific hemisphere in order to perform certain tasks. The right hemisphere is responsible for some elements of music, artistic creativity, rhyme, rhythm, patterns and emotions, while the left hemisphere has dominance for speaking, writing, calculation, sequence and analysis and is responsible for lines, lists, language and logic. This is not to say that each side controls these areas exclusively or are exactly the same in every person but that generally this is how these two domains operate. It was also discovered that the right hemisphere of the brain controls the motor functions of the left side of the body and vice versa.

In cases where the brain is not able for some reason to carry out its usual functions, for example where a person is deaf and therefore does not use the area usually allocated to hearing, this part of the brain may take over another use. In this particular case, the auditory processing part of the brain may, for example, take on a visual function resulting in a non-hearing person having greater visual skills than a hearing person.

Newborn babies can perceive speech slightly better with their right ear but distinguish musical tones with their left ear (right hemisphere), indicating that speech is a left brain activity and music generally is a right brain activity, although some aspects of music require left brain functions.

Music and language use both sides of the brain for the various functions involved in their processing. They are therefore ideal activities through which to exercise both hemispheres of the brain simultaneously. Sagan (1977) examined how the two sides of the brain have interacted to generate the accomplishment of our civilisation and believes that the effective pursuit of knowledge requires the collaborative functioning of both sides.

In 1745, there was a recorded case (by Carl Linnaeus) of a man who was paralysed down the right side of the body and suffered loss of speech, but could sing certain hymns that he had learned before his illness. Therefore, it was concluded that the right hemisphere controls singing whilst the left controls speech. There has been further evidence of this since. The condition whereby a person has difficulty with or is unable to use or understand language is termed 'aphasia'. People with this condition are often able to hum or sing.

I have witnessed myself a child under two years of age who was not yet speaking, but she could however vocalise a familiar tune, enunciating some of the words and performing the actions. I remember wondering how she could do this when she was not yet able to speak. The answer lies in the development of the different skills in different parts of the brain at different stages.

As music requires aesthetic and creative abilities whilst also requiring the appreciation of pattern and logic, it is possible that music can be used to engage both sides of the brain simultaneously. As rhythm, rhyme and patterns (governed by the right hemisphere) are important to reading and writing (governed by the left hemisphere), it would seem very likely that musical activities could stimulate the pathways in the brain to develop the skills required for successful reading and writing.

The response of the brain to music

With regard to the processing of music, the right side of the brain processes harmonic structure, quality and patterns of music, whilst the left side processes variance in volume, pitch and lyrics: both sides are required.

In a study by Cowell et al. in 1992, musicians were found to have more developed portions of the corpus callosum (the fibres joining the two halves of the brain). Schlaug et al. in 1995 confirmed this with their findings that classical musicians between the ages of 21 and 36 had a significantly increased size of the corpus callosum than their non-musical control. The significance of the increase in size of the corpus callosum is that, where it is larger there is increased capacity for the relaying of messages between the two sides of the brain. This may in turn account for the ability of music to aid memory function as confirmed in a study by Altenmüller et al. (2006). Essentially, musical training changes the structure of the brain. Musicians have more grey matter in the area of auditory and motor skills than their non-musical counterparts. (Grey matter is the grey-coloured tissue of the brain and spinal cord that contains nerve cells and blood vessels, as compared to white matter that consists of white-coloured myelin-coated nerve cell fibres. These carry information between the nerve cells in the brain and the spinal cord.) The significance of having more grey matter is that more nerve cells have formed so that there are more brain cells available for use!

When performing music, many parts of the brain are stimulated; motor activities are required. Reading music requires visual activity. It is important to listen to what is being played. The brain is required to link up these skills for the performance to be produced. Similarly, singing activates language areas of the brain as well as rhythmic and musical areas. Dancing or moving to rhythms stimulates the brain's motor areas. The fact that music necessitates the functioning of both sides of the brain is sufficient reason alone for children to be undertaking an increased amount of musical activities. That language and subsequently literacy may also utilise the same parts of the brain adds scientific argument to support the proposal that undertaking musical activities could greatly enhance a child's literacy potential.

In an interview of Weinberger by Dess (2000) for the journal *Psychology Today*, Weinberger suggests that long-term musical involvement reaps cognitive rewards in language skills, reasoning and creativity and boosts social adjustment – in effect, music exercises the brain.

Language processing in the brain

The first language that a baby hears is usually that of its mother. It will have become accustomed to the sound of her voice while in the womb. By the time that a baby is born, it is able to recognise the sound of her voice and other familiar sounds it may have heard whilst in the womb, music for example.

Babies learn about speech sounds by practising as well as listening. Talking requires the coordination of dozens of muscles in the lips, tongue, palate and larynx. The more response received by babies to their babbling, the more they will practise.

At the age of 6 months babies can recognise vowel sounds, and consonant sounds by 12–13 months (Werker and Lalonde, 1988). By 8 months, babies can recognise specific words (auditory recognition) up to two weeks after hearing them read repeatedly from a storybook (Eliot, 2000).

The Wernicke's area and Broca's areas of the brain are those specifically responsible for language processing. The Wernicke's area is responsible for processing the understanding of language and processing of vocabulary. It also helps the comprehension of non-verbal language, for example in identifying the sound of a train. This area of the brain develops before Broca's and is myelinated during the first two years. The Broca's area originally thought to be responsible for the production of speech is now also believed to process grammar.

In order for children to acquire language they must be exposed to it. In cases where children are deprived of language exposure or remain deaf to language for their early formative years, they can never acquire the language capabilities that they may have otherwise acquired. Grammar is particularly affected by late exposure. Babies who are born deaf will still babble initially. This then regresses as they are unable to hear their own babbling or other sounds with which to accord.

The second year of life seems to be the period when synapse formation and metabolic activity are at their height. This is the period when children develop major vocabulary growth. This explains the pace of language development from when children first enunciate words (vocabulary), up to the age of two years. They then begin to put the words together into a sentence (grammar).

From the age of two years, children begin to describe feelings, recite rhymes and their speech becomes more intelligible to strangers. By the age of four years, children have also acquired all of the basic rules of grammar to allow them to express themselves verbally.

When trying to learn a foreign language, although we may generally be able to pick up vocabulary reasonably easily if we are motivated, grammatical concepts often prove more difficult to assimilate as we get older. Pronunciation similarly can be difficult if we have not had early exposure to the sounds required. Similarly, learners of a foreign language are unable to speak like a native speaker unless exposed to the sounds of that language in their early years (preferably during the first six months).

To help children to learn foreign language sounds, encourage children to sing and play music from other countries. One song that you could try is this one in French, Claque, Claque. The translation is:

Clap, clap your knees, sleep like a fat owl

Swim like a big fish, fly like a butterfly.

To reinforce the words, add actions to complement the lyrics.

Eliot makes reference to a 'critical period' and believes that the critical window for language acquisition, when the brain has maximum capability for absorbing language, is up to the age of six or seven years (Eliot, 2000:. 363). The optimal part of the critical period is before the age of four.

Myelination appears between the ages of four and six years in the Broca's area. During this time children learn to put words in the correct order. They learn how to make plurals and describe events in the past, often with errors of agreement, such as 'I drawed' instead of 'I drew'. The connection between Wernicke's area and Broca's area, the 'arcuate fasciculus', is slow to myelinate which limits the speed of the development of grammatical accuracy (Eliot, 2000). This explains why such errors may continue until teenage years.

Between the ages of four and nine years, a child's brain is twice as active as an adult's brain. By the age of six, a child may have a vocabulary of 13,000 words, speak in sentences and be able to describe opposites but may still make grammatical errors. By the age of eight, most children are competent communicators; they can form complex sentences and carry out meaningful conversations with adults.

The interrelationship of music and language in the brain

It is actually difficult to separate completely the responses of the brain to music and language, as the two are so interrelated. Infants prefer **consonance** to **dissonance** and show preference for higher pitch. Higher pitch correlates with positive emotional judgements. This concurs with the higher pitch of 'motherese'. It is also more difficult for babies to pick up lower-pitched sounds. McMullen and Saffran (2004) also suggest that music sung by mothers to their babies is at a higher pitch than normal and generally consists of lullabies or play-songs.

Some parts of the brain respond similarly to linguistic and musical stimuli and the processing of language is thought to be similar to the processing of aspects of music. Some research has found that Broca's, an area of the brain that processes music, also deals with speech and language. Hence, the brain processes some areas of music in both sides of the brain. Research by Brown et al. (2006) considered 'Music and language side by side in the brain' and they found more parallels in their study of the generation of melodies and sentences.

Research by Sammler (2010) found that the brain processes music and lyrics together when hearing a song but then subsequently decodes the lyrics and treats the music separately. Brain scans show that music and language activate the same area of the brain, the superior temporal sulcus. The superior temporal sulcus is a groove that runs through the temporal lobe. Sammler's research showed that the middle part of this area processed the lyrics and the tune as a single signal but the anterior part of this area processed only the lyrics.

A related area of interest is that of stammering (distorting speech by blocks or interruptions of the rhythm). Whilst Gareth Gates, the TV *X Factor* runner up of December 2007 managed to sing beautifully, he was unable to speak without a stammer. This adds further weight to the evidence that singing and speaking are controlled by different areas of the brain. Whispering or speaking in chorus (chanting) are associated with singing and people do not stammer while doing either. Likewise, King George VI was helped by a speech therapist to overcome his stutter by, amongst other techniques, singing and chanting some of his sentences. This was portrayed in the film *The King's Speech* (2010), written by David Seidler.

This technique has received other evident success. Homan et al. (2005) found that music could help struggling readers. Using a software program originally developed to improve singing, Carry a Tune, Homan et al. studied its effect on reading fluency and comprehension. The program consisted of singing (karaoke style) to music, words that had to be read. The music's beat and flow helped pupils to become more fluent readers. The music also determined the pace and pupils were encouraged to maintain this pace of reading. Munro (in Masterson, 2000) found similar evidence that using the rhythm of a regular beat, such as clapping, helps the reader to progress at a regular pace. If children are already used to chanting and keeping a beat before they become readers then this will help them with reading at a later stage.

 Idea

The Bookstart website has online books to read along with children. The story *The Boy on the Bus* by Penny Dale is a sing-along story. The reader can follow the words and turn the pages of the book using the computer mouse.

Music, like language, stimulates many areas in the brain. The left planum temporale, a tiny area of the brain, is the area that enables the ability to recognise the pitch of a sound (it is a rare ability to be able to recognise exact pitch) and also plays an important part in the processing of language. It is also interesting to note that men have a larger planum temporale on the left side of their brains and use only this side to process language. However, women use the planum temporale on both left and right sides of the brain to process language. The larger planum temporale in men may well account for the better visual–spatial skills of men than women. Both the Wernicke's and Broca's are larger in women, both being used in language processing. This would suggest that females are generally better at language than males!

Aniruddh Patel's book *Music, Language and the Brain* (2007) is described on Amazon (online store) as the 'first comprehensive study of the relationship between music and language from the standpoint of cognitive neuroscience'. Patel argues that music and language share deep and critical connections. When we play or listen to music, many parts of the brain are activated:

Musical participation	Brain part activated
Listening	Auditory cortex
Reading music or movement	Visual cortex
Receiving vibration from an instrument	Sensory cortex
Movement, foot tapping, dancing and playing an instrument	Motor cortex
Movement and emotional reactions	Cerebellum
Creation and satisfaction of expectations	Pre-frontal cortex
Memory for music, musical experiences and contexts	Hippocampus

Patel suggests that music activates the language areas. For example, the Broca's area processes harmony, the way chords are put together in music and also syntax, the way in which words and sentences are structured.

In the *Grey Matters, From Molecules to Mind* UCSD TV series, in the edition Music and the Mind, Patel advises that music is ancient; a 35,000-year old flute has been discovered, suggesting that music maybe predates language. Patel suggests that music is important for the survival of the species. Music engages many brain functions such as emotion, memory, learning, attention, motor control, pattern perception and imagery. He suggests that music is both universal and unique to humans. People move to music. This is uniquely human – it is anticipatory in that we tap slightly ahead of what we know is coming. We can be flexible in that we can tap beats or a variety of rhythms. We can add accent if required in terms of a heavier or lighter beat. Responsible for this power of music over movement is the putamen, part of the basal ganglia that controls cognition, coordination and voluntary movement. It may also be responsible for aspects of learning and memory, habits in particular.

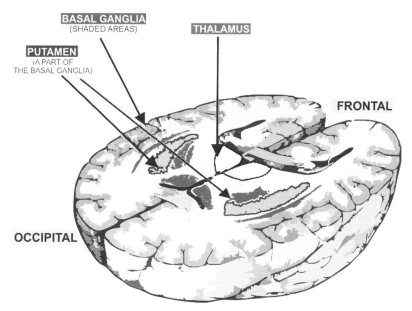

Figure 4.2   Horizontal Section of the Brain

Movement and the brain

Dr Maria Montessori, who was an Italian physician and educator, believed that children could absorb music in the same way that they absorb the language of their native land. She also thought that the 'Children should be seen and not heard' attitude towards children was misplaced. She believed that children would thrive best in an environment suited to their size and ability and where they could learn through doing. Whilst undertaking musical activities it is barely possible to remain stationary. Most pre-school musical activity involves some action rhymes. Clapping, stamping, dancing, playing instruments and moving to musical rhythms are the usual elements of a music session. The benefits of movement to learning have been examined by researchers, as there are those who believe that movement is required in order for us to stimulate the brain to learn. The impact of this should have profound effects on the school environment, where pupils are often expected to sit for many hours immersed in learning.

A child's natural movement to music is utilised in Dalcroze music teaching, where the method of using physical movements such as walking, running, hopping and skipping can be used to teach rhythm, rhythmic patterns and phrasing. These are also important elements of language. Movement can be used to demonstrate stresses, pauses, emphasis, duration and other aspects of language.

Eliot (2000: 155) reports a study of the effect of movement on babies' development. Babies aged 3–13 months old were subjected to sixteen sessions of being spun on a chair whilst sat on their parents' knees. The babies loved the treatment and showed advanced development of their reflexes and motor skills compared to control groups. This demonstrated that vestibular stimulation is good for the mind! The vestibular system is the sensory system that detects movement and helps to control balance.

If the vestibular system is over-stimulated then we may become nauseous. This is evidenced by car sickness and some people's inability to take rides on fairgrounds without feeling ill. Excessive movement can, of course, be extremely dangerous and cause damage to the brain!

It is well accepted that kinaesthetic learning (by movement and doing) assists in the acquisition and embedding of skills, hence singing, dancing and playing instruments will help to consolidate the learning of rhymes and songs. Learning by doing may well help to secure experiences in our memories as the physical act adds another dimension to the learning experience and may stimulate an increased number of synapses to make connections.

Movement may help us to feel good and create positive emotions. In response to movement the brain produces endorphins that make us feel good and this renders the brain more receptive to learning. Using both sides of the body uses corresponding sides of the brain, too, simultaneously exercising both. Feeling good helps us to function most effectively. Sarno (1998) and Hamilton (2005) write extensively on this subject.

Crossing the midline

A child needs to develop a dominant hand that crosses the midline so that it can perform bilateral activities. One hand must be dominant and the other supporting. If each hand is equally dominant so that neither needs to cross the midline, neither becomes strong and ability is limited. If dominance is not established, areas of difficulty may develop such as delayed language acquisition, poor gross and fine motor skills and difficulties with comprehension and organisation.

Many daily activities require **bilateral coordination** such as drawing a line with a ruler, threading, eating with a knife and fork and clapping. Both hands are required to cooperate in order to complete the task. Playing a musical instrument requires both hands and therefore requires the brain to coordinate the work of both sides.

The process of establishing a dominant side of the body is termed **'lateralisation'**. This is an important process, as once established the right and left hemispheres of the brain communicate to allow 'bilateral coordination' – the cooperation of both sides of the body. A prerequisite to lateralisation is the ability to 'cross the midline'.

Activities 4.2, 4.3 and 4.4 help to practise bilateral coordination.

Activity 4.2   Simon Says (game)

This popular party game is played with one player taking the role of Simon. Simon then gives instructions to the other players. The last player to perform the action is 'out'; the last player remaining is the winner. By giving instructions for actions which cross the midline you can help children to practise bilateral coordination. For example, 'Simon says – reach to the left' or 'reach to the right'. Other instructions could include 'cross your feet, cross your arms or touch your left ear with your right hand.'

 Activity 4.3   Copy the Sound (bilateral coordination activity)

The teacher makes a sound on an instrument and passes it round the children in turn. Each child has to make the same sound, in the same way as Chinese Whispers. Ensure that children then use both hands to pass the instrument on; this will ensure that they cross the midline.

 Activity 4.4   Beat the Drum (bilateral coordination activity)

With a beater in each hand, children play a drum that the teacher holds up to the left and right, alternately. The children have to play it to the left with the right hand and vice versa – ensure that the arms cross over the midline. The teacher can determine how many beats are to be played at each side.

Playing instruments and clapping help children to develop fine motor skills and using actions that cross the midline helps to promote bilateral coordination.

In order to write, cross-lateral movement is required – that is the ability to move a pen across a page, as the arm will move across to the other side of the body. Activities using gross motor skills where bilateral coordination is required help children to practise these skills. These include movements where limbs need to cooperate in order to complete the action such as marching, jumping, tiptoeing or running. The next activity, Stamping, helps children to practise gross motor skills.

Sing the song Stamping whilst stamping and playing the beat on a drum. The teacher then asks the children, 'How else could you move?' This is then incorporated into the song, for example, skipping, running, hopping, jumping, tiptoeing or even walking sideways. The teacher plays slowly or quickly, according to what suits the action. Children could take turns to be the leader with the drum.

Movement and language

Movement can help to consolidate language. Encouraging children to move in the manner suggested by rhymes and songs helps to embed vocabulary. Campbell and Brewer (1999: 20) draw links between movement and language and state that movement and rhythm stimulate the frontal lobes that are important in language development.

Both hemispheres of the brain can be stimulated by movement. The activities performed at music sessions involve moving and/or dancing to music and necessitate left and right side of the body actions – ideally if these can be performed simultaneously then this may help the development of future reading skills.

A popular activity for pre-school children is marching to the song The Grand Old Duke of York. Verses can be adapted so that the Duke and his men could stamp up the hill in hobnail boots or tiptoe in soft pink slippers! This activity stimulates the imagination, language abilities and physical skills.

Activity 4.6   The Grand Old Duke of York (song)

Sing whilst marching along to this rhythm and playing along with instruments, too, playing the instruments up in the air when the men march 'up' and playing them down near the ground when the men are 'down'.

Lyrics: Trad.

Trad.
Arr. M. Kay

Oh the Grand Old Duke of York   he   had ten thou-sand men,   He

marched them up to the top of the hill and he marched them down a - gain,   And

when they were up they were up   and when they were down they were down,   And

when they were near - ly   half way up they were nei - ther up   nor down!

The rhyme can be varied to replace the word 'men' with that of any animal or vehicle and then a description of how it might go. For example, the men – marched, horses – galloped, mice – scampered, rabbits – jumped, rockets – zoomed, boats – floated. Children could make suggestions as to what and how something went up the hill.

Memory

The hippocampus (Greek for seahorse), so called due to its shape, is located in the temporal lobe in each side of the brain. It is part of the brain that is involved in memory formation and processes long-term memory. It is most effective when we are active. The hippocampus also helps to consolidate new memories and transfers them from short- to long-term memory. It helps us to know where we are. This is known as 'spatial orientation'. It also has some responsibility for emotions. The hippocampus makes associations between places and sounds and connects to other memories. If it is damaged, a person may remember the distant past but not form new memories.

Movement can help to embed information into the memory (Voss et al., 2011). Making associations also helps the brain to store information (Buzan, 2006). A part of the brain that is responsible for the processing of both movement and memory is the putamen, which is situated in the basal ganglia. This may well account for a link between movement and memory.

Repetition

I believe that learning is best embedded by repetition, repeated exposure and regularity of task performance. A way to enhance '**rote learning**' is to set drills to music. Stories, rhymes and songs that we have heard many times may be easily recalled, sometimes even in to the latter years. My grandmother (at the age of 91) was able to recall French vocabulary that she had learned at school over 75 years previously. Since leaving school at the age of 15, she never visited France or used the French language. The vocabulary had been drilled and regularly revisited at school and hence it stayed entrenched in her memory and she was able to recall it over 80 years later! Such is the importance of early experience and the establishment of sound foundations.

Summary ☐

This chapter has considered how the brain develops. It must initially be stimulated in order to make the connections necessary for future processing. Failure to stimulate the brain results in loss of connections. The remaining connections can be strengthened throughout life but we cannot make new ones. The most important time in life for forming these initial connections is before three years of age.

Evidence from this chapter has revealed that the brain uses both hemispheres in the processing of music and language. Melodies and sentences use the same parts of the brain in their processing.

This chapter has also investigated how movement can help the brain. When we dance to music, both sides of the brain are used to control our motor activities and also to take in what we are hearing. Hence moving to music stimulates the brain. Playing an instrument requires the use of both sides of the brain as it necessitates the use of motor and cognitive skills, simultaneously.

Something to think about

- Introducing songs, rhymes and music from other countries into your children's repertoire helps them to learn other languages later in life. The rhythms in language are reflected in the music of its country. Think about the music that you could include in your sessions that might help later language learning.

- When working with young children, observe and monitor their ability to use one hand to support the other. Encourage activities that require the cooperation of both hands.

Something to read

Eliot, L. (2000) *What's Going on in There? How the Brain and Mind Develop in the First Five Years of Life*. New York: Bantam Books.

Useful websites

http://www.ot-mom-learning-activities.com – learning activities to help with motor skills, hand dominance and midline crossing

http://www.bookstart.org.uk – sing-along stories and other activities on the 'Have some fun' tab (accessed June 2012)

http://www.youtube.com/watch?v=GHb_aqP4JgY – a discussion about 'The Power of Rhythm' from Sacks' book *Musicophilia* may be listened to on YouTube, along with other interesting stories from this book (accessed April 2012)

http://www.youtube.com/watch?v=ZgKFeuzGEns – the video entitled Music and the Mind is from the series *Grey Matters*. In this video, Aniruddh Patel discusses amongst many other things, musical and language grammar and explains how the human brain helps us to maintain a beat

5

The way forward: literacy through music

This chapter covers

- Ideas to literacy-enrich music sessions

- Advice for structuring a pre-school literacy-through-music session

- Advice for the delivery of a session

- Example of a pre-school literacy-through-music session (30–40 minutes)

- More activity ideas for primary-aged children

- Musical stories

- Ideas for children with additional support needs

In order to facilitate the acquisition of the skills that will be required later for literacy through musical activities, it is necessary to focus on literacy outcomes. From the information in Chapter 1, it is apparent that participation in musical activities may reap many benefits, but as advised in Chapter 2, in order to assist literacy development musical activity alone is not enough. There must be a deliberate intention to optimise all opportunities to foster literacy skills which is integral to delivery. The emphasis must be on HOW the activities are presented such that literacy outcomes are elicited.

Some ideas to help to literacy-enrich musical activities are listed below. The ideas are presented to correspond with the early learning goals of the 'communication and language' and 'literacy' areas of learning and development of the EYFS Statutory Framework for the Early Years Foundation Stage (DFE, 2012a). Many activities will overlap the sections.

Ideas to literacy-enrich music sessions

Suggestions for songs or rhymes and their activity numbers in this book are provided in brackets for ease of reference.

Communication and language early learning goals

Listening and attention:

- Use children's names in songs (Hello, Activity 5.1).

- Include songs relating to letter sounds (What Does This Letter Say?, Activity 2.1).

- Be aware of tone and intonation. Vary the sounds made and emphasise them. Enunciate clearly.

- Use props and puppets to focus attention.

- Encourage children to recognise and identify the voices of your puppets before they are visible.

- Listen to sounds from other languages. For example, the BBC website CBeebies has *The Lingo Show*, which encourages children to listen and to speak words of other languages. There are many sites with songs in other languages (for example, http://www.mamalisa.com).

- Include activities to encourage the development of auditory discrimination skills – detection of changes in pitch (Slide Whistle, Activity 3.3) and timbre appreciation (Sound Pairs, Activity 5.2).

- Encourage children to maintain the beat of songs through body movements or the use of instruments, encourage them to stamp loudly or tiptoe quietly, matching their movements to their or your voice.

- Ask children to clap or tap on a drum the syllables of their names or answers to a question (Syllables, Activity 3.1).

- Encourage children to listen for matching sounds at the beginning and end of words.

- Ask children how they might make a similar sound to, for example, a squirrel cracking nuts, a galloping horse – which instrument would they choose? Tell a story where the 'sound effects' are required. Experiment by making body, vocal and instrumental sounds to create sound effects.

- Encourage children to 'listen' to differences in sound. Ask 'Which instrument am I playing?' with the instrument inside a box out of sight, or 'Which animal makes this sound?' after playing a recorded animal sound. (Match Sounds to Their Sources, Activity 2.5 and Sound Pairs, Activity 5.2.) Collect 'sound' resources for these activities.

- Take turns to make or copy a sound.

- Encourage children to suggest new rhyming words for rhymes and songs.

Understanding:

- Encourage understanding of syllabification by playing or clapping the rhythms of songs together.

- Include musical stories and ask questions such as, 'What happened at the end?' and 'What happens next?'.

- Help children to learn new concepts or lists by singing them (Days of the Week, Activity 1.6).

- Encourage children to make suggestions and incorporate their ideas into the songs.

- Encourage learning about the world (Creepy, Crawly Caterpillar, Activity 1.10).

- Encourage children to talk about their experiences.

- Encourage children to reason and consider consequences – pose the question 'Why?'.

- Use rhymes and songs that tell stories (Wee Willie Winkie, Activity 3.2), give instructions (If You're Pleased and You Know It, Activity 1.9), and help children to learn about structure (It's Time to Put the Instruments Away, Activity 1.7).

Speaking:

- Use any opportunity to ask questions and encourage discussion, for example when hearing a sound, ask the children to determine the source and ask, 'What does it look like?' Talk about how sounds are made.

- Encourage children to use different voices and at differing pitches and volumes (What Does a Mouse Say?, Activity 2.2).

- Use puppets to encourage children to respond – encourage conversation.

- Sing songs and recite rhymes in other languages (Mi Gorro Tiene Tres Picos, Activity 1.2 and Claque, Claque, Activity 4.1).

- Encourage children to express emotions appropriately and at appropriate times (If You're Pleased and You Know It, Activity 1.9).

- Encourage focus and concentration by singing in rounds (I Hear Thunder, Activity 1.5).

- Encourage social interaction using rhymes that require turn-taking and cooperation.

- Use signing for songs or instructions to support vocal instructions (try British Sign Language, Baby Signing or Sing and Sign). See instructions for My Hat It Has Three Corners (Activity 1.1).

- Incorporate and stress 'onomatopoeia' (I'm an Elephant, Activity 2.6).

- Use body language, facial expression and sign language to support speech (Mi Gorro Tiene Tres Picos, Activity 1.2).

- Use repetition; practising speech helps children to embed the sounds in their memories.

- Use call-and-response rhymes and songs to encourage conversational technique (Hello, Activity 5.1).

Literacy early learning goals

Reading:

- Ensure where possible that the note values in any music match the syllables in the lyrics of songs.

- Encourage children to match sounds with pictures or **realia** of what may make the sound.

- Show letters of the alphabet to children and ask them to match the sound with the symbol.

- With alliterative jingles or rhymes (Five Fat Flies, Activity 2.3), ask the children to identify the sound or letter and ask for suggestions for other words matching initial or final sounds.

- Encourage children to develop sequencing skills by repetition of rhymes, songs and stories.

- Complement an on-going theme with choice of songs. For example, pirates, transport, animals, weather, festivals, celebrations, seasons.

- Ask children to make different sounds on their instruments and to play loudly and softly, slowly and quickly (I Hear Thunder, Activity 1.5).

- Sing songs from written text once children are able to read, to encourage fluency of reading.

- Sing songs from text before children are able to read to help them to behave like readers and to help them to begin to recognise the patterns and direction of text.

- Sing stories to demonstrate that songs and texts have meaning and structure.

- Omit rhyming words at the end of rhymes for the children to supply them (Wee Willie Winkie, Activity 3.2).

- Make use of alliteration – as puppet names or in rhymes.

- Giving puppets an alliterative name is fun and also helps the child to remember the name, for example Mollie Minim, Terry the Tiger, Singing Suzie. Placing a deliberate accent on the first sound of the name and lengthening it also helps children to learn initial sounds, for example Ssssammy, Sssssnake.

- Use storybooks/alphabet books when presenting music to enhance bibliographic knowledge.

Writing:

- Encourage children to use their imaginations.

- Help to embed memory by the use of actions.

- Encourage the development of bilateral coordination skills through games, rhymes and songs that require gross motor skills.

- Supply a good range of sturdy instruments to enable children to practise a variety of fine motor skills.

- Encourage children to write giant letters or practise making shapes in the air – use a rhyme such as Can You Make a Circle? (Activity 2.7).

- Use props. Use claves for tapping rhythms. Use puppets to accompany rhymes. Use building bricks to support rhymes and help to develop coordination skills (Building Bricks, Activity 2.8). Use ribbons or scarves to accompany rhymes, and use to link children together, to dance or to take an imaginary dog for a walk.

- Write new lyrics to traditional melodies to complement themes. Make up your own songs or rhymes to tell stories.

Advice for structuring a pre-school literacy-through-music session

Suggested structure:

- 'Hello' song – include the names of the children.

- Alphabet and concept rhymes.

- Rhymes using props.

- Moving around.

- Circle rhymes.

- Instruments.

- Action rhymes and rhymes in other languages.

- Closing songs.

- 'Goodbye' song.

Incorporating a variety of activities ensures that young children maintain focus and interest and that there is something for everyone. This structure is one that I have used for many years and it works well as children learn to anticipate what is coming next and enjoy the activity changes. For parents with a baby, there are activities that can be enjoyed with a baby on the parent's knee and when the older children are moving around I find that parents are happy to join in carrying their babies around, too. I begin with everyone sitting on chairs, then some activities sitting on the floor, such as rowing. Following this, I include activities where the children can run around being animals or transport, ending with animals sleeping or transport stopping so that there is control at the end of the activity. After the activities with instruments, the session then begins to draw to a close with a few more action songs and the final 'Goodbye' song.

Include three or four musical activities in each category plus the 'Hello' and 'Goodbye' song. If you have around thirty short songs or rhymes you will have plenty to choose from for a 30–40 minute session. Initially it is a good idea to use fewer songs and to repeat each song until the children become familiar with the actions and words. Ensure that the programmes are consistent. Children enjoy being able to anticipate what is coming next. New activities can be introduced gradually and may be themed or reflect the season.

When structuring a musical session for pre-school children it is important for the children to know when the session is starting and when it is ending, so always using the same 'Hello' and 'Goodbye' songs is recommended. Use a simple and repetitive tune that is easy to learn and remember.

A suggestion is the song entitled 'Hello'.

If you are playing recorded music to sing along to, try to ensure that the songs have an introduction so that you and the children can anticipate the beginning of the song and know when to begin singing. Using well-known tunes or simple tunes encourages participation. Traditional songs are ideal as they have already stood the test of time.

Advice for the delivery of a session

- Before the sessions, practise singing the words and performing the actions.

- Ensure that your instruments are safe for all children.

- Sing slowly initially, to enable children to hear and learn the words.

- Use plenty of short songs with lots of repetition of words and melody – these are easy to use and fun; children will soon join in.

- Use actions to support the lyrics to songs.

- Use colourful puppets and props to add interest to sessions and encourage interaction.

- Vary the activities so that some time is spent, for example, sitting, standing, moving, playing instruments and using props.

- Include children's names in the 'Hello' and 'Goodbye' songs.

- Be aware of the literacy outcomes you are addressing and help to focus the children's attention on them.

- Use an alphabet book to teach sound–symbol correspondence of initial letter sounds.

- Repeat the same activities in the same order each time so that the children may become familiar with the sequence. They will enjoy being able to predict what is to come.

- When the pupils are participating and enjoying the activities, gradually introduce some new ones.

- Don't worry if everyone doesn't join in. Children can be assimilating everything around them even when they appear not to be participating at all.

- Keep going, don't stop for interruptions.

BE ENTHUSIASTIC AND ENJOY THE SESSIONS YOURSELF!

Example of a pre-school literacy-through-music session (30–40 minutes)

Many of the activities throughout this book are incorporated in this example programme.

'Hello' song:

- Hello song (Activity 5.1).

Alphabet and concept rhymes:

Alphabet rhymes:

- Alphabet Song (sing the letters of the alphabet to the tune of 'Twinkle Twinkle Little Star').

- What Does This Letter Say? (Activity 2.1).

- Five Fat Flies (Activity 2.3).

Knowledge of the world:

- Days of the Week (Activity 1.6).

- Creepy Crawly Caterpillar (Activity 1.10).

- Wee Willie Winkie (Activity 3.2).

Floor/Props (use finger puppet mice):

- Mouse, Mouse (Activity 2.4).

- What Does a Mouse Say? + verses for other animals (Activity 2.2).

Floor:

- Building Bricks (Activity 2.8).

Moving:

- Can You Make a Circle? Use ribbons or scarves (Activity 2.7).

Play music and encourage the children to move and draw in the air to it; encourage them to draw straight lines, circles and tails, as in writing.

Alternatively, elect a leader to make a shape and let the others copy the shape. Suggest some shapes that are to be used first, such as a square, circle or triangle. The other children have to watch carefully to see which one is being written.

- Can You Tiptoe? (Activity 1.8).

- Stamping (Activity 4.5).

- Simon Says (Activity 4.2).

Circle rhymes:

- If You're Pleased and You Know It (Activity 1.9).

- I'm an Elephant (Activity 2.6).

Instruments:

- Slide Whistle (Activity 3.3).

- Match Sounds to Their Sources (Activity 2.5).

Encourage the children to learn the names of different instruments, for example the guiro, agogo and cabasa:

- Syllables (Activity 3.1).

- Pass round a drum and copy rhythms (a variation of Activity 3.1).

- Beat the Drum (Activity 4.4).

- I Hear Thunder (Activity 1.5). This may also be sung in a round.

- Pedro, Pedro (Activity 5.3).

- I Like to Eat Bananas (Activity 5.4).

- Musical story – there is a section on musical stories later in this chapter.

- The Grand Old Duke of York (Activity 4.8).

- It's Time to Put the Instruments Away (Activity 1.7).

Action rhymes and rhymes in other languages:

- My Hat It Has Three Corners + signing + in Spanish (Activities 1.1, 1.3 and 1.2).

- Claque, Claque (Activity 4.1).

Closing songs:

- Bingo (Activity 1.4).

- Autumn in Scotland (Activity 5.5).

'Goodbye' song:

- Goodbye.

This can be the same melody as the Hello song and similarly include the children's names.

More activity ideas for primary-aged children

Most early years settings offer some form of musical sessions. Given the increasing body of research extolling the merits of using music to enhance literacy skills development, these should be increasing.

Music is a natural part of the Montessori curriculum. Maria Montessori was a proponent of experiential learning. She set up her own school in 1906 in Rome. The Montessori method of teaching is based on the belief that children are naturally inquisitive and will teach themselves if given the right environment and materials.

The Montessori system uses its own musical equipment. One example of equipment is the Montessori bells. The purpose of the bells is to introduce children to the discrimination of musical sounds by pairing and ordering. Two identical sets of bells in the scale of C Major are provided. Children can pair the bells by sound and place them in the correct order of pitch by playing them and listening to the sounds that they make. This could be achieved with any two sets of hand bells.

 Activity 5.2   Sound Pairs (auditory discrimination activity)

Another exercise to help auditory discrimination is to make pairs of sound makers for children to match. For example, I collected the small, black containers that used to hold camera film. Inside the containers I placed dried peas/beans, paper clips, rice, paper, nothing, a wooden ball and dried lentils. Then I made another identical set. Children can pair the containers by shaking them and matching them by the sounds that they make.

Alternatively, the teacher can give containers to the children and retain a matching set. The teacher makes a sound with one container and each child, in turn, has to identify when their container has the same sound as the one that the teacher is holding.

Extending the activities already mentioned to elicit more advanced skills could include:

- Children sing a song and add their own endings or substitute new lyrics, for example use the traditional tune of Twinkle, Twinkle, Little Star and write lyrics on a given theme, for example a favourite pet, such as the one in Activity 5.3. I refer to songs with substituted words as 'subs'.

 Activity 5.3   Pedro, Pedro (song)

Pedro, Pedro, little cat

Black and white and a little bit fat

Lazing, lazing, all day long

Wait a minute, I may be wrong

Pedro, Pedro, little cat

He's caught not a mouse but a great big rat!

Lyrics: M. Kay

- Children read the lyrics whilst singing (this helps fluency of reading).

- Identification of **homonyms** and **homophones**.

- Listen to a piece of music and write a story telling what the music is about.

- Children in pairs can sing words with two or more syllables to each other, one child leads and the other mimics the sounds as closely as possible. They could use a xylophone to sound out the syllables before singing. They could try differing intervals.

- Sort instruments into categories of materials, such as wood, metal, plastic, or you may even find some vegetable casings such as those made from squash, for example, an African-made Cabasa. Describe the differences in the types of sounds that they make.

- Select instruments from Africa or India and discuss what they are made of. Compare these instruments to others from Europe; discuss the similarities and differences in terms of materials, sounds and uniformity of size and shape.

Musical stories

Songs often tell stories. There are songs available to accompany traditional fairy tales such as *Goldilocks and the Three Bears* or *The Sleeping Beauty*. Songs for these stories and others may be found in the book *Sing Me a Story*, details of which are at the end of Chapter 2.

We're Going on a Bear Hunt by Michael Rosen is a retold classic story with a strong rhythm for children to march or clap along to. Props can be used to emulate the wavy grass (cheerleader pompoms), swirling snowstorm (fan and water), mud (wellies). Alternative lyrics for landscapes can be invented to suit the props that you have available.

Mick Inkpen's book *The Blue Balloon* offers scope for imagination. Children can have a balloon each and see how many different sounds they can make with it. Children could suggest sound effects as they follow the journey of the blue balloon as the story is read to them. They could imagine being the balloon and how it would feel being inflated and deflated; this could lead on to further discussion about what makes things grow and what materials stretch. If the children were balloons, where would they fly to and how would they move? They could spin or rise quickly or drop, or just float.

Based on Pat Hutchins' *Good-Night, Owl!* make a model owl with eyes that open and close. Use whatever you have to make noisy sounds. For example, I change the story so that a squirrel, a horse, a thunderstorm, a train, the school bell, children and a woodpecker make so much noise that they wake up Ollie the Owl each time he tries to sleep. I use a cabasa and/or guiro for a squirrel sound, drums and rainmaker for a thunderstorm, coconut shells or castanets for a galloping horse, a train whistle for a train, bells and triangles for a school bell, lots of instruments together for school children and long-handled castanets for a woodpecker. Each child contributes their sound effect at the appropriate point in the story, whilst the leader operates the eyes on the owl. These animals or events wake up the owl as he tries to sleep. This activity helps children to listen, predict and participate.

An excellent book that includes a story of travelling around the world, rhyme, onomatopoeia, syllabification and colourful illustrations is *In Search of Sounds* by Miriam Moss. It also has suggestions for thinking about and making sounds to accompany the story, plus games and ideas to generate movement to sound.

Ideas for children with additional support needs

Most of the activities suggested so far can be used or easily adapted for use with all children. For older children, it is important that the programme content is suitable to their level of maturity. Where activities require the playing of instruments, an alternative could be to use claves. These may be easier to hold and operate than other instruments; they could be used for tapping out beats and rhythms. This encourages the development of motor skills.

- An idea to help children with the discrimination of sounds is to make recordings of sounds in the environment and take photos of the source of the sound, for example a creaking door, a washing machine, a 'singing' toy, running water, printer, doorbell, telephone. Play a game where the sounds are matched with the photos. Alternatively children could record their voices; they could describe themselves or their hobbies. When playing back the recordings, the children would have to identify the voices. They could include older and younger voices and compare the differences.

- Where children have hearing impairments then they may need to feel the vibrations of sound or have the item generating the sound put close enough for them to perceive it. Musical activities can be multi-sensory. When telling a story about the seaside, for example, record sounds of the sea, seagulls, dolphins; make textured pictures to be 'read' alongside the story. The textures could have sand in the paint for the beach, cottonwool clouds, cellophane sea, pieces of seaweed and driftwood, a towel, shiny paper fish, rubbery dolphins and a shell could be attached by string. Take care that the pieces do not easily fall or are easy to pick off. A fan could help to create a windy scene. A story about a jungle could include the sounds of the animals and the rustling trees. There are many sound effects that may be easily downloaded from the Internet.

- In order to include musical experiences that cover all of the senses, songs could be included about food and their respective flavours. In the exercise I have described previously of beating out syllables on a drum that is passed round a group, the subject for the syllabification could be food. One child could say and tap the syllables of their favourite food and the next child could tap out their opinion or description of that food, including its aroma. Aromatic filled containers could be offered to the children and they could describe the various smells. Suggestions for olfactory experiences include ginger, pepper, peppermint essence, almond flavouring, strawberry flavouring, citrus juice, tea tree oil and lavender. This exercise could be the basis for a song. For example, Activity 5.4. These lyrics may be sung to the melody of Carnival of Venice (as for My Hat It Has Three Corners).

 Activity 5.4   I Like to Eat Bananas (song)

I like to eat bananas, I do like tangerines

But eating my school dinner makes me shiver and makes me squeam!

Lyrics: M. Kay

In addition to aiding memory and stimulating the imagination this would also help to enhance a child's vocabulary.

- Activities that involve crossing the midline provide good exercises in coordination, so these are to be encouraged if possible. Moving both hands to the left and to the right encourages bilateral coordination.

- A parachute could be used if the children can hold and move one. Use the parachute to consolidate concepts such as left and right, up and down, in and out.

- Activities need to be relevant for the target age group but most songs can easily be adapted by a simple change of lyrics. Whilst undertaking the topic of 'Autumn' with a group of children, I found videos to show them of autumnal activities in Scotland. These included salmon and trout fishing, dolphin watching and work in the forest. I wrote the lyrics of Autumn in Scotland and set them to a traditional Scottish melody. The song is easy to sing due to its repetitive lyrics and the catchy tune. The rhythm of the music changes in each verse to reflect the syllables in the words. I use BSL signs for actions to accompany the song.

Activity 5.5   Autumn in Scotland (song)

Lyrics: M. Kay

Trad.
Arr. M. Kay

Summary

This chapter offers a culmination of the activities detailed throughout the book, along with advice on the structure and presentation of a literacy-enriched music session. The session presented is ideal for pre-school children but can be adapted by the substitution of some of the other activities offered for use with older children.

(Continued)

(Continued)

Music can provide a means of expression. It can be as energetic or as passive as required. Tailor the activities to the abilities of the children and to the outcomes that you wish to achieve.

There is a wide variety of resources available for the presenting of musical activities to children in books, government publications and on the Internet. Being aware of the skills necessary for success in literacy is the first step to designing a literacy-through-music programme. Having decided on the skills that you wish to promote, select activities that will help children to practise these skills. Repeat activities that the children enjoy and that achieve the outcomes desired.

Something to think about

- Think about the outcomes that you wish to achieve and the activities that you would feel comfortable presenting. Choose activities that you could maybe enhance with the use of puppets or ones that particularly fit in with topics that you may currently be presenting.

Something to read

These books offer ideal stories for adding sound effects as the story is read or they can provide a basis for an adapted story to fit the sound effects that you have available.

Hutchins, P. (1990) *Good-Night, Owl!* New York: Aladdin Paperbacks.
Inkpen, M. (2006) *The Blue Balloon*. London: Hodder Children's Books.
Moss, M. (2008) *Chiff Chaff and Chickpea: In Search of Sounds*. London: Youth Music.
Rosen, M. (1993) *We're Going on a Bear Hunt*. London: Walker Books Ltd.

Useful websites

http://www.funmusicco.com – ideas for teachers.
www.bussongs.com – lots of free lyrics, videos and music for children's songs and rhymes
www.nancymusic.com – music for children and information about music and literacy

Conclusion

Participating in musical activities endows young children with a myriad of far-reaching benefits, not least those affecting language and subsequently literacy. Storr (1992: 64) states that: 'Music can best be understood as a system of relationships between tones, just as language is a system of relationships between words.' This relationship between music and language is the reason that each can be used to enhance and enrich the other. The same skills are utilised in both areas.

The existence of such close parallels between music and literacy suggests that it would be sagacious to undertake musical activities with all pre-school children at home and in educational settings. Drawing a child's attention to differences in sounds helps to foster phonological awareness and helps with later phonics comprehension. By focussing musical activities such that literacy elements are elicited, it is possible to build many of the skills that will later secure success in literacy.

Unlike 'readiness to read' there can be no discrepancy as to when children are ready to receive music. Musical activities can be undertaken from birth. Hence the inclusion of music in any early years programme is invaluable.

The importance of early exposure to a stimulating environment cannot be overstated, as it is in these early years that the brain is forming and supporting the development of the body's systems. Listening to and participating in musical activities at an early age helps to embed sounds and structures that will later be used for language.

Participation in musical activities offers children opportunities to practise oral skills. Through an awareness of and an ability to process sound, children are able to develop the skills that enable them to communicate through listening and speaking. Once these skills are acquired children learn to encode and decode the sounds in graphic form. It is imperative that the former precedes the latter – sound before symbol. Musical activities can support and nurture this relationship in a way that is almost osmotic.

For primary children music offers a rich resource through which to deliver much of the literacy and other areas of the curriculum. Literacy skills continue through our school lives and beyond. Without basic literacy skills the ability to learn in other areas is severely disadvantaged. Music provides a natural and inclusive form of communication that can facilitate speech development and confidence.

The neural pathways in the brain can be stimulated through music. The greater the stimulation that the brain receives the more connections it is able to establish. It is important to maintain these connections through continued use. Music is an ideal medium through which to exercise the brain, as musical activities require the cooperation of both left and right hemispheres. Repetition such as that required to learn rhymes and songs also helps to reinforce and embed memories for life.

Research in many areas is proliferating since the advent of brain imaging. This has enabled scientists to pinpoint areas that are activated when particular activities are undertaken. Scientists are also able to understand more about how processes are carried out by the brain. The availability of research relating to music, language and the brain enables greater insight into links between these areas to be gained.

As recognition of the significant value of early exposure to music gains weight, an increasing number of projects are being funded such as that by the NLO, described at the end of Chapter 3. Another project in Scotland, funded by the government agency Creative Scotland, proposed for twelve months, after October 2012, to give up to 60,000 families with newborn babies a free classical CD. This project aimed to inspire a love of music and to assist cognitive development (Simpson, 2012: 8).

There are many excellent pre-school music programmes available, but the use of these to promote literacy development could be extended. I believe that music provision for children needs to be given a more prominent role and that it should pervade all areas of learning. Music should be pivotal to the curriculum and not be regarded as peripheral, as is its current status.

Without suggesting that music is a panacea, the evidence herein suggests that it can certainly help to facilitate language and literacy development. An increase in music provision throughout education can only serve to facilitate the success of pupils in many areas and ultimately to aid the advancement and prosperity of society.

Glossary

Alliteration   The repetition of a particular sound in the first syllables of consecutive words or phrases. For example, 'The silver snake slithered over the slimy sludge.'

Amusia   The condition of not being able to recognise music or reproduce it.

Amusic   A person suffering from the condition 'amusia'.

Analogy   A similarity between like features on which a comparison may be based. For example, a heart and a pump.

Analytic phonics   Words are analysed (taken apart) by using phonics as a clue for decoding. Children identify a phoneme by making analogies to those that they already know. For example, they recognise that the initial sound in 'pig' is the same as the initial sound in 'pen'.

Aphasia   The condition whereby a person has difficulty with or is unable to use or understand language.

Arhythmic   Lacking rhythm or regularity of rhythm.

Audiation   The process of mentally hearing and comprehending music that is not physically present.

Auditory discrimination   The ability to detect differences between sounds.

Bibliographic knowledge   Knowing how to read a book and how to find information in it.

Bilateral coordination   The ability to use both sides of the body at the same time. It requires the communication of both sides of the brain.

Blend   A blend is letters placed together to make a sound. A consonant blend consists of two or three consonants, for example 'sl' as in 'slip' or 'spr' as in 'spring'.

Classical (Pavlovian) conditioning   An association is made between a stimulus and a response. For example, a bell to signify mealtime.

Consonance   A combination of notes that sound pleasant when played at the same time.

Control group   A group that acts as a reference whereby the experiment applied is not applied to that group, so that the effects of both can be compared.

DCSF   Department for Children, Schools and Families (2007–10).

DFE   Department for Education (2010–).

DfEE   Department for Education and Employment (1995–2001).

DfES   Department for Education and Skills (2001–07).

Digraph   A pair of letters representing a single sound. A consonant digraph would be, for example, 'sh', 'ch', 'th', 'wh', 'ck', 'ph'; a vowel digraph would be, for example, 'ai', 'ee', 'ea', 'oa'.

Dissonance   A combination of noises that sound harsh or unpleasant when heard together.

Duration   The time length of a musical sound or note.

Dynamics   The loudness or quietness of sound.

Emotional literacy   The ability to recognise, understand and appropriately express emotions.

Entrancement   To be delighted; fascinated; to go into a trance.

EYFS   Early Years Foundation Stage – a statutory framework specifying standards for the development, learning and care of children from birth to five years of age in England.

Grammar   The rules governing the composition of language.

Grapheme   The written symbol representing a sound. For example, 'ph'.

Homologous   Having corresponding features.

Homonym   Words with the same spelling and pronunciation but different meanings. For example, bank (verb or noun), left (past tense of 'to leave' or the opposite direction to right). These are also homophones as they sound the same. A homonym that is spelt the same but pronounced differently. For example, live (verb or adjective) is only a homonym.

Homophone   Words that sound the same. They may have different meanings and spellings. For example, boar/bore, which/witch.

Inner hearing   Playing and hearing music inside the head when it is not actually being played.

Internalise   Incorporate within oneself.

Interval   The distance in pitch between two musical notes.

Intervention   A supplementary programme – in the case of reading, to help increase reading levels.

Lateralisation   This is the term for the process of developing dominance of one side of the body for physical functions. For example, becoming right-handed.

Metacognitive knowledge   Knowledge of one's own thought process.

Metre   The pattern of beats in music or poetry. In music it refers to recurring measures in note lengths and bar lengths and in poetry to the arrangement of syllables in a line and lines in a verse. It also refers to the stressed accents on notes or words. Metre describes the recurring rhythms.

Motoric   Imparts motion.

Myelin   An insulating substance that forms a sheath around the brain cells. This sheath then conducts electrical signals from the brain to the body.

Onomatopoeia   A word that suggests the source of the sound that it describes. Examples include, 'thud', 'tap', 'splash' and 'tick-tock'.

Onset   The part of the syllable that precedes the vowel in a word. For example, 's' in 'sit'.

Phoneme   The smallest unit of sound that conveys a meaning. There are more than 40 of them in the English language. For example, 'th'.

Phonemic awareness   The ability to hear and identify phonemes.

Phonics   The method of teaching reading whereby pupils are taught to match language sounds with the corresponding letters or groups of letters. For example, 'd' for dog.

Phonological awareness   The ability to perceive the sound structure of words.

Phonological memory   The ability to remember sounds in words.

Pitch   The degree of highness or lowness of a sound.

Plastic   Capable of being changed or adapted.

Plasticity   The ability to change and adapt.

Productive vocabulary   Words we use when we speak or write.

Realia   Real life objects such as a real dog as opposed to a picture of a dog.

Receptive vocabulary   Words that we understand when we hear or see them.

Rime   The part of the syllable that consists of its vowel and any consonant sounds after it.

Rote learning   A memorisation technique based on repetition.

Round   A musical composition in which singers sing the same song but beginning at different times.

Structure   The way that individual parts are put together.

Subvocalise   Articulate without making sound, as when reading to oneself.

Syllable   A segment of sound in a word, for example syl-la-ble (3), dog (1) Jan-u-a-ry (4).

Synapse   The junction of space between two nerve cells.

Syntax   The study of the rules governing how words work together to form phrases, clauses and sentences.

Synthetic phonics   Synthesising (combining) sounds to make words, for example c-a-t. It is used predominantly on regular spellings.

Tempo   The speed of a piece of music.

Texture   This describes the different ways in which sounds are combined. Music with a single melody line is thin and simple in texture; music with many parts and layers may be thick and complex.

The oneness of one   The concept that the number 'one' represents one item.

Timbre   The type or quality of sound.

Vestibular   The sensory system detecting movement and helping to control balance.

Viewing   Visual discrimination, the ability to recognise and identify visual shapes, forms and patterns.

Viewing skills   Being able to gain meaning or a message from a visual image.

References

Adams, M.J. (1990) *Beginning to Read: Thinking and Learning about Print*. Cambridge, MA: The MIT Press.

Allen, G. (2011) *Early Intervention: The Next Steps: An Independent Report to Her Majesty's Government*. London: Cabinet Office.

Allen, R.E. (ed.) (1990) *The Concise Oxford Dictionary of Current English*. Oxford: Oxford University Press.

Altenmüller, E., et al. (2006) *Music, Motor Control and the Brain*. Oxford: Oxford University Press.

Berke, M. (2008) 'From the chair', *General Music Today*, 21(2): 5.

Blumenfeld, H. and Eisenfeld, L. (2006) 'Does a mother singing to her premature baby affect feeding in the neonatal ICU?', *Cinical Pediatrics*, 45: 65–70.

Bolduc, J. (2008) 'The effects of music instruction on emergent literacy capacities among preschool children: a literature review', *Early Childhood Research & Practice (ECRP)*, 10 (1), available at: http://www.ecrp.uiuc.edu/v10n1/bolduc.html (accessed May 2012).

Brierley, J.K. (1994) *Give me a Child Until he is Seven: Brain Studies and Early Childhood Education*. Abingdon: RoutledgeFalmer.

Brown, S. (2001) 'Are music and language homologues? The biological foundations of music', *Annals of the New York Academy of Sciences*, 930: 372–4.

Brown, S., et al. (2006) 'Music and language side by side in the brain: a PET study of the generation of melodies and sentences', *European Journal of Neuroscience*, 23: 2791–2803.

Burling, R. (2007) *The Talking Ape: How Language Evolved*. Oxford: Oxford University Press.

Buzan, A. (2006) *Use Your Head*. Harlow: Pearson Education Group.

Campbell, D. and Brewer, C. (1992) *Rhythms of Learning*. Cheltenham, Victoria: Hawker Brownlow Education.

Carlisle, R. and Wendon, L. (1992) *The Letterland ABC*. Dorking: Templar Publishing Ltd.

Cassidy, S. (2010) 'Should under-fives be taught to read and write?', *The Independent*, 4 November, available at: http://www.independent.co.uk/news/education/schools/should-underfives-be-taught-to-read-and-write-2124637.html?printService=print (accessed May 2012).

Coldwell, M., et al. (2011) 'Process evaluation of the Year 1 Phonics Screening Check Pilot', *Research Brief*, DFE-RB159, available at: http://www.education.gov.uk/publications/eOrderingDownload/DFE-RB159.pdf (accessed August 2012).

Cook, G. (1995) *Note Reading for Young Children*. Vilonia, AR: Noteimals LLC.

Cowell, P.E., et al. (1992) 'A developmental study of sex and age interaction in the human corpus callosum', *Developmental Brain Research*, 66: 187–92.

Cowling, K. and Cowling, H. (1993) *Toe by Toe*. Baildon: K and H Cowling.

D'Agrosa, E. (2008) 'Making music, reaching readers making powerful connections possible for young students', *General Music Today*, 21 (2): 6–10.

Darrow, A. (2008) 'Music and literacy', *General Music Today*, 21 (2): 32–4.

Department for Children, Schools and Families (DCSF) (2007) *Letters and Sounds: Principles and Practice of High Quality Phonics Notes of Guidance for Practitioners and Teachers*. Nottingham: DCSF Publications.

Department for Children, Schools and Families, (DCSF) (2008) *Statutory Framework for the Early Years Foundation Stage*. Nottingham: DCSF Publications.

Department for Education (DFE) (2011a) *The Framework for the National Curriculum: A report by the Expert Panel for the National Curriculum review*. London: DFE.

Department for Education (DFE) (2011b) *The Importance of Phonics: Securing Confident Reading, Evidence Paper.* London: DFE.

Department for Education (DFE) (2012a) *Statutory Framework for the Early Years Foundation Stage 2012.* London: DFE, available at: http://www.education.gov.uk/schools/teachingandlearning/curriculum/a0068102/early-years-foundation-stage-eyfs (accessed May 2012).

Department for Education (DFE) (2012b) *Statutory Programme of Study for Key Stage 1 and 2 Music.* London: DFE, available at: http://www.education.gov.uk/schools/teachingandlearning/curriculum/primary/b00199150/music (accessed May 2012).

Department for Education (DFE) (2012c) *Statutory Programme of Study for Key Stage 1 and 2 English.* London: DFE, available at: http://www.education.gov.uk/schools/teachingandlearning/curriculum/primary/b00198874/english (accessed May 2012).

Department for Education and Employment (DfEE) (1998) *The National Literacy Strategy: Framework for Teaching.* London: DfEE.

Department for Education and Employment (DfEE) (2001) *The National Literacy Strategy: Developing Early Writing.* London: DfEE.

Dess, N.K. (2000) 'Music on the mind', *Psychology Today*, 33 (5): 28, September, available at: http://www.psychologytoday.com/articles/200008/music-the-mind (accessed May 2012).

Doman, G. (1988) *Teach Your Baby to Read.* London: Pan Books Ltd.

Douglas, S. and Willatts, P. (1994) 'The relationship between musical ability and literacy skills', *Journal of Research in Reading*, 17 (2): 99–107.

Dryden, G. and Vos, J. (2005) *The New Learning Revolution*, 3rd edn. London: Continuum International Publishing Group.

Early Education (2012) *Development Matters in the Early Years Foundation Stage (EYFS).* London: Early Education.

Eliot, L. (2000) *What's Going on in There? How the Brain and Mind Develop in the First Five Years of Life.* New York: Bantam Books.

Foorman, B., Fletcher, J. and Francis, D. (1997) *A Scientific Approach to Reading Instruction.* Learning Disabilities Online, available at: http://www.ldonline.org/article/6251 (accessed October 2012).

Galliford, J. (2003) 'The effects of music experience during early childhood on the development of linguistic and non-linguistic skills', doctoral dissertation, University of Miami, Miami, FL.

Gardner, H. (1985) *Frames of Mind: The Theory of Multiple Intelligences.* New York: Basic Books.

Goddard, S. (2002) *Reflexes, Learning and Behavior: A Window into the Child's Mind.* Eugene, OR: Fern Ridge Press.

Gordon, E.E. (1979) *Primary Measures of Music Audiation.* Chicago, IL: GIA Publications.

Goswami, U. (1997) 'A reason for rhyme', *Times Educational Supplement*, 21 March, p. 12.

Goswami, U. and Bryant, P. (1990) *Phonological Skills and Learning to Read: Essays in Developmental Psychology.* Hove: Psychology Press Ltd.

Hamilton, D.R. (2005) *It's the Thought that Counts.* Hamilton: Bonnybridge.

Hansen, D., et al. (2004) *The Music and Literacy Connection.* Reston, VA: MENC: National Association for Music Education.

Heald, C. and Eustice, V. (1988) *Ready to Read.* Leamington Spa: Scholastic Publications Ltd.

Henley, D. (2011) *Music Education in England – A Review by Darren Henley for the Department for Education and the Department for Culture, Media and Sport.* London: DFE.

Holliman, A.J., et al. (2010) 'The contribution of sensitivity to speech rhythm and non-speech rhythm to early reading development', *Educational Psychology: An International Journal of Experimental Educational Psychology*, 30 (3): 247–67.

Homan, S.P., et al. (2005) 'Does singing improve reading skills? Using unique "learn-to-sing" software with struggling middle school readers', *Research Abstract*, November. Tampa, FL: University of South Florida, available at: http://www.tuneintolearning.org/pdf/ResearchAbstract_I.pdf (accessed May 2012).

Horne, M. (2011) 'Benedetti burn-out', *The Scottish Mail on Sunday*, 17 July, p. 30–1.

Johnston, R. and Watson, J. (2005) 'The effects of synthetic phonics teaching on reading and spelling attainment: a seven-year longitudinal study', *Insight 17*. Edinburgh: IAC: ASUSchools, available at: http://www.scotland.gov.uk/Publications/2005/02/20682/52383 (accessed August 2012).

Jordan-DeCarbo, J. (2006) 'Research review: can a systematic and age-appropriate music curriculum raise test scores for preschool children?', *Perspectives Journal of the Early Childhood Music and Movement Association*, 1 (4).

Kay, A.M. (1997) 'Sound before symbol', MA dissertation, University of East Anglia.

Kjaer, K. (1993) 'A development programme based on musical stimulation – target group 6 months to 3 years', Seminar Paper, *PRESMA Newsletter*, No. 30.

Kokas, K. (1969) 'Psychological testing in Hungarian music education', *Journal of Research in Music Education*, 8 (3): 102–14.

Kozminsky, L. and Kozminsky, E. (1995) 'The effects of early phonological awareness training on reading success', *Learning and Instruction*, 5 (3): 187–201.

Kraus, N. and Chandrasekaran, B. (2010) 'Music training for the development of auditory skills', *Nature Reviews Neuroscience*, 11: 599–605.

Lamb, S.J. and Gregory, A.H. (1993) 'The relationship between music and reading in beginning readers', *Educational Psychology*, 13 (1): 19–27.

Lazarev, M. (2010) Mamababy: *Birth Before Birth*. North Charleston, SC: CreateSpace.

Learning Point Associates (2004) 'A closer look at the five essential components of effective reading instruction: a review of scientifically based reading research for teachers', Naperville, IL: Learning Point Associates, available at: http://www.learningpt.org/pdfs/literacy/components.pdf (accessed May 2012).

Lloyd, S. (1992) *The Phonics Handbook*. Chigwell: Jolly Learning Ltd.

Logan, B., et al. (1994) 'Brave New Babies', *Equinox*, Sunday 20 November, 1994, Television Channel 4.

Longfellow H.W. (1835) *Outre-Mer: A Pilgrimage Beyond the Sea*, Vol. 2. New York: Harper and Brothers.

Lonie, D. (2010) 'Early years evidence review, assessing the outcomes of early years music making', London: Youth Music, available at: http://www.youthmusic.org.uk/assets/files/Early%20years%20evidence%20review%202010(2).pdf (accessed May 2012).

Machin, S. and McNally, S. (2004) *The Literacy Hour*. London: Centre for the Economic of Education.

Masterson, K. (2000) 'With a simple tune, students improve in school', Educational CyberPlayground, available at: http://www.edu-cyberpg.com/Culdesac/ReadingModule/Munro.html (accessed May 2012).

McMahon, O. (1979) 'The relationship of music discrimination training to reading and associated auditory skills', *Bulletin of the Council for Research in Music Education*, 59: 68–72.

McMullen, E. and Saffran, J.R. (2004) 'Music and language: a developmental comparison, music perception', 21 (3): 289–311.

Meek, M. (1982) *Learning to Read*. London: Bodley Head Ltd.

Meredith, D. (1998) 'Look East', BBC Television, April.

Mizener, C.P. (2008) 'Enhancing language skills through music', *General Music Today*, 21 (2): 11–17.

Moyeda, I.X.G., et al. (2006) 'Implementing a musical program to promote preschool children's vocabulary development', *Early Childhood Research and Practice*, 8 (1), available at: http://www.ecrp.uiuc.edu/v8n1/galicia.html (accessed May 2012).

Moyle, D. (1968) *The Teaching of Reading*. London: Ward Lock Educational.

National Institute of Child Health and Human Development (2000) *Teaching Children to Read: An Evidence-Based Assessment of the Scientific Research Literature on Reading and its Implications for Reading Instruction* (NIH Publication No. 00-4569). Washington DC: US Government Printing Office, available at: http://NationalReadingPanel.org/publications/publications.htm (accessed October 2012).

Norman, J. (2011) 'Sing up and break the silence', *The Sunday Times*, 10 July, available at: http://www.jesse4hereford.com/content/sunday-times-sing-and-break-silence (accessed April 2012).

94   SOUND BEFORE SYMBOL

Oldham, G.R., et al. (1995) 'Listen while you work? Quasi-experimental relations between personal-stereo headset use and employee work responses', *Journal of Applied Psychology*, 80 (5): 547–64.

Patel, A. (2007) *Music, Language and the Brain*. Oxford: Oxford University Press.

Paton, G. (2010) 'Children more likely to own a mobile phone than a book', *The Telegraph*, 26 May, available at: http://www.telegraph.co.uk/education/educationnews/7763811/Children-more-likely-to-own-a-mobile-phone-than-a-book.html (accessed May 2012).

Piro, J.M. and Ortiz, C. (2009) 'The effect of piano lessons on the vocabulary and verbal sequencing skills of primary grade students', *Psychology of Music*, 37: 325.

Register, D. (2001) 'The effects of an early intervention music curriculum on prereading/writing, *Journal of Music Therapy*, 38 (3): 239–48.

Rose, J. (2006) *Independent Review of the Teaching of Early Reading: Final Report*. Nottingham: DES Publications.

Roskam, K.S. (1993) *Feeling the Sound: The Influence of Music on Behavior*. San Francisco, CA: San Francisco Press, Inc.

Sagan, C. (1977) *The Dragons of Eden: Speculations on the Evolution of Human Intelligence*. New York: Ballantine Books.

Sacks, O. (2008) *Musicophilia: Tales of Music and the Brain*. London: Picador.

Sainsbury, M. (1997) 'Test group slips under the baseline', *Times Educational Supplement*, 7 February, available at: http://www.tes.co.uk/article.aspx?storycode=146823 (accessed May 2012).

Sammler, D. (2010) 'The relationship of lyrics and tunes in the processing of unfamiliar songs: a functional magnetic resonance adaptation study', *Journal of Neuroscience*, 30 (10): 3572–8.

Sarno, J.E. (1998) *The Mind Body Prescription*. New York: Warner Books.

Savan, A. (1999) 'The effect of background music upon learning', *Psychology of Music*, 7 (2): 138–46.

Schlaug, G., et al. (1995) 'Increased corpus callosum size in musicians', *Neuropsychologica*, 33 (8): 1047–55.

School Curriculum and Assessment Authority (SCAA) (1997a) *Looking at Children's Learning: Desirable Outcomes for Children's Learning on Entering Compulsory Education*. London: SCAA.

School Curriculum and Assessment Authority (SCAA) (1997b) *Music and the Use of Language*. London: SCAA.

Schreckenberg, G. and Bird, H.H. (1987) 'Neural plasticity of musculus in response to disharmonic sound', *The Bulletin*, New Jersey Academy of Science, 32 (2): 77–86.

Seidler, D. (2010) *The King's Speech*. Momentum Pictures.

Shaw, G.L. (1999) *Keeping Mozart in Mind*. San Diego, CA: Academic Press.

Shore, R. (1997) *Rethink the Brain: New Insights into Early Development*. New York: Families and Work Institute.

Simpson, J. (2012) 'Nutcracker sweet: classical CD for every bably, *The Times*, 12 October, p. 8.

Sloboda, J.A. (1989) *The Musical Mind: The Cognitive Psychology of Music*. New York: Oxford University Press.

Smith, F. (1978) *Understanding Reading: A Psycholinguistic Analysis of Reading and Learning to Read*. London: Holt, Rinehart and Winston.

Smith, F. (2004) *Understanding Reading: A Psycholinguistic Analysis of Reading and Learning to Read*, 6th edn. Mahwah, NJ: Lawrence Erlbaum Associates.

Smith, R. (2012) 'Sound of silence', *Daily Mirror*, 9 March, p. 27.

Standards and Testing Agency (STA) (2012) *Assessment Framework for the Development of the Year 1 Phonics Screening Check*. London: DFE, available at: www.education.gov.uk/publications (accessed October 2012).

Standley, J.M. and Hughes, J.E. (1997) 'Evaluation of an early intervention music curriculum for enhancing pre-reading/writing skills', *Music Therapy Perspectives*, 15: 79–85.

Stansell, J.W. (2005) 'The use of music for learning languages: a review of the literature', available at: http://www.mste.illinois.edu/courses/ci407su02/students/stansell/Literature%20Review%201.html (accessed May 2012).

Storr, A. (1992) *Music and the Mind*. London: Harper Collins.

Strait, D.L., et al. (2011) 'Subcortical processing of speech regularities predicts reading and music aptitude in children', *Behavioral and Brain Functions*, 7: 44, available at: http://www.behavioralandbrainfunctions.com/content/7/1/44 (accessed May 2012).

Taylor, H. and Clark, J. (2007) *Turning their Ears On … Keeping their Ears Open*. London: Youth Music.

Thomas, S. (1997) 'Early years: a tale of two classes', *Times Educational Supplement*, Issue 2, 31 January.

Torgerson, C.J., et al. (2006) 'A systematic review of the research literature on the use of phonics in the teaching of reading and spelling', *Research Report No. 711*, Nottingham: DfES Publications.

Van der Gaag, A. (1999) *The Early Communication Audit Manual: A Talking Toolkit*. London: Royal College of Speech and Language Therapists, available at: http://www.literacytrust.org.uk/talk_to_your_baby/about (accessed May 2012).

Vinken, P.J. and Bruyn, G.W. (eds) (1969) *Handbook of Clinical Neurology*, Vol. 4. Amsterdam: North-Holland Publishing Company.

Voss, J.L., et al. (2011) 'Hippocampal brain-network coordination during volitional exploratory behavior enhances learning', *Nature Neuroscience*, 14 (1): 115–20.

Walters, C. (2012) 'School music under threat', *The Guardian*, 16 April.

Webb, T.W. and Webb, D. (1990) *Accelerated Learning with Music: A Trainer's Manual*. Norcross, GA: Accelerated Learning Systems.

Welch, G., et al. (2011) *A Research Evaluation of the New London Orchestra 'Literacy Through Music' Programme*. London: International Music Education Research Centre (imerc), Institute of Education, University of London.

Werker, J. and Lalonde, C. (1988) 'Cross-language speech perception: initial capabilities and developmental change', *Developmental Psychology*, 24: 672–83.

Wiggins, D.G. (2007) 'Pre-K music and the emergent reader: promoting literacy in a music-enhanced environment', *Early Childhood Education Journal*, 35 (1): 55–64.

Winkler, I., et al. (2009) 'Newborn infants detect the beat in music', *Proceedings of the National Academy of Sciences*, 106 (7): 2468–2471, available at: http://www.pnas.org/content/106/7/2468.full (accessed May 2012).

Index